How to Receive
the Holy Ghost

How to Receive the Holy Ghost

Francine Harris

Copyright © 2019 by Francine Harris.

Library of Congress Control Number: 2019900331
ISBN: Hardcover 978-1-9845-7634-7
Softcover 978-1-9845-7633-0
eBook 978-1-9845-7632-3

All rights reserved. No part of this book may be reproduced or transmitted in any form or by any means, electronic or mechanical, including photocopying, recording, or by any information storage and retrieval system, without permission in writing from the copyright owner.

The views expressed in this work are solely those of the author and do not necessarily reflect the views of the publisher, and the publisher hereby disclaims any responsibility for them.

Scripture quotations marked KJV are from the Holy Bible, King James Version (Authorized Version). First published in 1611. Quoted from the KJV Classic Reference Bible, Copyright © 1983 by The Zondervan Corporation.

Any people depicted in stock imagery provided by Getty Images are models, and such images are being used for illustrative purposes only. Certain stock imagery © Getty Images.

Print information available on the last page.

Rev. date: 10/29/2019

To order additional copies of this book, contact:
Xlibris
1-888-795-4274
www.Xlibris.com
Orders@Xlibris.com
786131

Contents

Chapter 1	The Operation of the Holy Spirit Before the Birth of Jesus Christ	1
Chapter 2	The Symbolic Meanings of the Mosaic Laws	6
Chapter 3	Understanding the Mosaic Law	18
Chapter 4	Why You Should to be Baptized in the Name of the Lord Jesus Christ	30
Chapter 5	What is Sanctification?	37
Chapter 6	The Power of Fasting and Prayer	57
Chapter 7	The Different Operations of the Holy Spirit	70
Chapter 8	The Importance of Being Filled with The Holy Ghost	79
Chapter 9	The Upper Room Experience in the Book Acts	85
Chapter 10	My personal Testimonies and Supernatural Experiences	96

Biography 107

Chapter 1

The Operation of the Holy Spirit Before the Birth of Jesus Christ

We see in Exodus the 19th chapter that the children of Israel were in Mount Sinai which was a desert place.

God spoke to Moses and told him to tell the people that he was coming down in a thick cloud in the mist of them, and that they were to sanctify themselves for his appearance.

The lord told Moses to also tell them to wash their clothing and to not come at their wives. This was a part of their sanctification process.

After reading the text you would wonder why God would allow the people to go through all of this in the first place? One thing that we have to remember is that God has a Holy nature and cannot allow sin to be in his presence. On the other hand, we are not righteous enough to go directly into his presence because of this. This is the reason that Jesus is our mediator between God and man.

*But we are all as an unclean thing, and all our righteousness are as filthy rags; and we all do fade as a leaf; and our iniquities, like the wind, have taken us away. **(Isaiah 64:6)KJV***

First let, me explain to you what a mediator is the natural realm and then in the spiritual as well. In the natural world a mediator, is a link between people in order to bring about an agreement or reconciliation.

The definition that I just gave you would be used for the natural world, moreover the type of mediator that Jesus represented was for the spiritual realm.

Jesus told the disciples in St John the 14th chapter to not let their hearts be troubled. He had only given them a hint to what he was about to go through on the cross, and therefore he didn't go into great details at that particular time. Furthermore, he told them that he was going away, but they couldn't come yet. In addition, one of his disciples whose name was Philip saith unto him, Lord shew us the father, and it sufficeth us.

Jesus saith unto him, Have I been so long time with you, and yet hast thou not known me, Philip? he that hath seen me hath seen the Father; and how sayest thou then, Shew us the Father? **(John 14:8) KJV**

You have to keep in mind that the natural world is ran differently than the spiritual world. On the other hand, the bible is not a natural book. The reason that we don't see more miracles and Gods power like in biblical the days is, because we are too caught up into this worldly system and in our fleshly desires.

Thomas saith unto him, Lord, we know not whither thou goest; and how can we know the way? Jesus saith unto him, I am the way, the truth, and the life: no man cometh unto the Father, but by me. **JOHN 14:5**

In addition, man can also be a mediator for others, but man was not worthy enough to die for the entire world, because we were born in state of sin and shaped in iniquity. **(Palms 51) KJV**

Jerimiah 31:33 But this shall be the covenant that I will make with the house of Israel; After those days, saith the Lord, I will put my law in their inward parts, and write it in their hearts; and will be their God, and they shall be my people.

This scripture is telling us that Jesus was a mediator for a new covenant because God was not satisfied with the old one that was under the Mosaic Law.

Under the Mosaic Law the animal was used as the sacrifice for the sins of the people. But under the new covenant Jesus was the perfect sacrifice that was crucified for our sins.

The meaning of the word covenant in the natural world would be an agreement, a pledge, or a promise, but of course, in the spiritual world the word would be an agreement between God and Man.

After Noah and his family had left the ark, he decided to build an alter unto the Lord. Therefore, he took some of the clean animals and used them for a burnt offering as unto the Lord. As a result, God was well pleased with the aroma from the burnt offerings.

God also made a covenant with Noah and his family. In addition, he established the covenant with his seed and the animals as well. Of course, most people are aware that he was talking about Abraham and the Israelites.

Therefore, the Lord would not destroy the earth with water neither by a flood again. Consequently, God decided that he would place a rainbow in the clouds for a token because of this. The covenant was also given to the creatures that lived on the earth. Furthermore, he also said that this covenant would last forever. **(Genesis 9:8)**

When God made a covenant with Abraham, he was ninety years old. Therefore, this particular covenant was not just for Abraham but for his seed as well.

In addition, the Lord changed Abrahams name on the same day that the covenant was made. His name was changed from Abram to Abraham.

What was in the covenant that was made with Abraham? First, all of the males had to be circumcised on the eighth day after they had been born under the Mosaic Law. This part of the covenant was classified as a token of the covenant that God had made.

The second thing that God told Abraham is that his wife's name would be changed from Sarai to Sarah, and that she would bare a son in her old age. Moreover, Sarah was ninety-nine years old when Isaac was conceived, and Abraham was a hundred. The Lord said that she would be the mother of many nations; and kings of people would come from her seed. **(Genesis 17)**

Also, the reason these patriarchs are so important is because they were the beginning, or the foundation used on the earth to be used by God for the redemption of man. In addition, Jesus Christ was called the son of David because he was a part of his genealogy. **(Romans 1:3)**

Finally, we know that the words of God are true, because every word that was spoken by God and the true prophets came to pass and was fulfilled after it had been spoken.

*God is not a man, that he should lie; neither the son of man, that he should repent: hath he said, and shall he not do it? or hath he spoken, and shall he not make it good? **(Numbers 23:19)KJV***

Sarah Abraham's wife bare him no children. Therefore, an angel also came and prophesied to her and stated that she would conceive and bare a son in her old age. Sarah was ninety years old at the time this took place.

Moreover, the prophecy came to pass at the exact timing that the angel had stated that it would. But before this had taken place Sarah suggested that Abraham would go into her maid, whose name was Hagar which was an Egyptian, so that she could conceive for her.

During biblical times having children was a very special event for a woman, especially for females that bore male children as well. In addition, the first-born son would usually receive the inheritance from the family.

Remember, that you can relate natural things to the spiritual realm, so that you can get a better understanding about what I am trying to convey to you in this book.

Why would God call Israel his first born?

Now these are the names of the children of Israel, which came into Egypt; every man every man and his household came with Jacob.

Reuben, Simeon, Levi, Judah, Issachar, Zebulun, and Benjamin, Dan, and Naphtali, Gad, and Asher.

God sends Moses to give a warning to Pharaoh. He tells him to tell him to let his son go, that they may serve him. But if he refused then he would kill his first-born son as well.

I guess you're wondering what Abraham's genealogy was. First, Abraham and Hagar bore Ishmael. After this Abraham and Sarah bore Isaac. Then Isaac and Rebecca bore Jacob and Esau. And Jacob bore the twelve tribes of Israel.

The names of Jacobs sons were Reuben, Simeon, Levi, Judah, Zebulun, Issachar, Dan, Gad, Asher, Naphtali, Benjamin, and Joseph. **(Genesis 49)KJV**

There mother's names were Leah, Rachael, Bilhah and Zilpha. Moreover, Bilhah and Zilpha were both maids of Rachael and Leah. **(Genesis 30:1-14)KJV**

Some people may not be aware of this, but the twelve tribes of Israel will be written on the gates in heaven. There will be three names on the east, three names on the north, three names on the south, and three names on the west. Furthermore, there will be twelve foundations and the twelve Apostles names will be written in them as well. **(Revelation 21:9:13) KJV**

Hagar Sarah's maid finally conceived and bore a son just as Sarah had hoped for, because she desired to have a child. But conflict took place between Hagar and Sarah after the conception of the child. Therefore, Hagar fled into the wilderness because of this. As a result, the angel of the Lord met her in the wilderness and told her what to name her son.

And the angel of the Lord said unto her, Behold, thou art with child, and shalt bear a son, and shalt call his name Ishmael; because the Lord hath heard thy affection. And he will be a wild man; and his hand will be against every man, and every man's hand against him; and he shall dwell in the presence of his brethren. **(Genesis 16:11-12) KJV**

Sometimes in life God will allow us to go into the wilderness. Why? First, so that he can get our attention, because we are sometimes too comfortable in this life. Second, this is one of the ways that he sometimes test us when we are his child, so that we may know what is in our hearts. And third this is another way that we can be made in the fire so that we can come out as pure gold. As a result, he can also reveal to us as what his will is for our lives. In fact, trouble is not always as bad as it may appear. However, it all depends on how you view what God is doing in your life.

For whom the Lord loveth he chasteneth, and scourgeth every son whom he receiveth.

If ye endure chastening, God dealeth with you as with sons; for what son is he whom the father chasteneth not? **(Hebrew 12:6)KJV**

You have to remember that Ishmael's mother was an Egyptian, and she therefore had some of the traits of her forefathers, which consisted of idolatry and other evil acts that God was not pleased with. Therefore, it would not be a surprise that Ishmael would be born a wild man because of his genealogy. However, Ishmael was not the promised child, because it had been spoken by the angel to Abraham that Isaac would be the one that was chosen by the Lord.

Chapter 2

The Symbolic Meanings of the Mosaic Laws

For the law was given by Moses, but grace and truth came by Jesus Christ. (John 1:17)KJV

God wanted a new covenant because he was not pleased with the old one. He said that he was tired of the animal scarifies, and that he would bring a new covenant as well.

In the book of Genesis Abraham had asked God would he spare Sodom and Gomorrah because he was going to bring judgement on those two cities?

The reason that the Lord was allowing judgment to take place in those cities is because the sins, of the people. In fact, their sins were so great that it had reached the throne of God. Therefore, God had to put a stop to the madness.

This is an example of what can happen when a nation or a person turn their backs on God and pushes him away. This does not mean that everyone will give their lives to him, but when we began to reject him and turn away from him, this can be a very dangerous thing for a nation. He knows that we were born in sin and shaped in iniquity, but there is a such thing as crossing the line whereby, judgment could take place as well.

Because sentence against an evil work is not executed speedily, therefore the heart of the sons of men is fully set in them to do evil. **(Ecclesiastes 8:11) KJV**

In the Old testament when people sinned the judgement of God took place right away, but under grace, Gods judgments will take place at the end. Therefore, because people believe that they are getting away with their evil deeds they sometimes may become more comfortable, which could cause their hearts to become harder. This means that the things that once bothered them may not have the same effect as it once did in the past.

*Every way of a man is right in his own eyes: but the Lord pondereth the hearts. **(Proverbs 21:2) KJV***

Consequently, the Lord told Abraham if he could find ten righteous people in Sodom and Gomorrah that he would spare these two cities. But they could not be found. Therefore, the Lord brought great judgement on them.

This also, lets us know that God will sometimes spare a nation or a person if there are a few righteous people, that may be seeking his face. Therefore, this is an example of someone that has a relationship with God. They therefore, can stand in proxy for someone else's sins.

There are many testimonies of people who have had miracles to take place in their lives, by the power of God. Some people never would've made it without God's help. Others were at death doors or could have lost their minds.

What makes a powerful testimony? Sometimes people's backs are against the wall and they need a supernatural deliverance. Furthermore, you can't have a testimony without a test.

Notice, I stated in the beginning of the chapter that the Israelites had to sanctify themselves, before approaching Mount Sinai or coming near it. The word sanctification is not a popular word in these last and evil days. Because when you sanctify yourself that means that you have to be more than just a church goer and you must surrender yourself totally to the Lord. In addition, sanctification is a very important for our spiritual growth, and it helps us to be more Christ like.

Under the Mosaic Law the tribe of Levi were responsible for the upkeep of the tabernacle. On the other hand, there were three parts to the tabernacle. (Levi was the son of Jacob and Leah)

The tabernacle consisted of the Outer Court,

the Holy Place, and the Holy of Holies.

The tabernacle was a place where God dwelt under the Mosaic Law, but under grace our bodies are now the new temple that Christ would like to dwell.

*[9] What? know ye not that your body is the temple of the Holy Ghost, which is in you, which ye have of God, and ye are not your own? **(1st Corinthians 6:19) KJV***

Flee fornication. Every sin that a man doeth is without the body; but he that committeth fornication sinneth against his own body. ***(1ˢᵗ Corinthians: 6-18) KJV***

Brazen Alter

Another name for the brazen alter would be the bronze alter or the Alter of Burt offering. It was located in the Outer Court of the tabernacle under the Mosaic Law. But it was the first piece of furniture that you saw when you entered the court yard and was also made out of Acai wood. However, it was five cubits long and three cubits in height. Furthermore, the shape of the Brazen Alter was square. (**Leviticus 1:1-14) KJV**

Only the Levites were allowed to work in the tabernacle. The Levites were the offspring of Levi which were Jacob and Leah's son. But they were also a part of Abraham's seed.

Moreover, the Brazen Alter was used for the sacrifices for their sins of the Israelites. In other words, the animal was sacrificed for the sins of the person. In addition, the animal had to be perfect and could not have any blemishes.

They were allowed to bring bulls, goat, sheep, and pigeons. However, if the person was poor, they could bring pigeons or fine flour mixed with oil for their sacrifices as well.

This piece of furniture was symbolic for the way that our Lord and Savior Jesus Christ had been crucified for our sins. In addition, it was symbolic for how he blead, suffered and died for the sins of the entire world. **Exodus27**

If you notice the animals had to be perfect and could not have any blemishes. However, Jesus was the perfect sacrifice and there was no guile or sin found in him. In addition, this is one of the reasons that the animals had to be perfect. Because, it was symbolic for what was to come under the New Covenant. On the other hand, there was not a man on earth that was qualified to die for the sins of man. Because Jesus was not conceived by an earthly father, and was not born with an adamic nature, he was therefore, able to die for the sins of the entire world. **(Matthew 1:18) KJV**

The people would come to the temple every day, with an animal for the atonement for their sins. But Jesus died to cleanse our sins and give us power over our fleshly desires. Furthermore, he only had to die once for our sins not repeatedly. Moreover, in Hebrews the 9th chapter it mentions how Jesus became a high priest and was the perfect tabernacle that was not made by hands.

He also became a mediator for us under the New Testament.

For there is one God, and one mediator between God and men, the man Christ Jesus. (1st Timothy 2:2-6) KJV

Remember that I stated that we are not holy enough to go directly to God, because of his holy nature. This is one reason that the scripture says that he became a mediator for us. **(Hebrews 9:11-15) KJV)**

The Bronze Laver

The Bronze Laver was also located in the outer court of the tabernacle.

This particular piece of furniture was made from the mirrors that the Israelites, or the women had gotten from the Egyptians, when they left Egypt. The Bronze Laver resembled a large basin and it contained water.

The Laver was used for the priest to wash their hands and feet before entering the tabernacle. Moreover, if they went into the tabernacle and didn't obey the instructions that the Lord had commanded them, they could drop dead.

The reason for this is because God cannot tolerate sin, nor can it be in his presence.

The Bronze Laver was also symbolic for the New covenant. Finally, it symbolized the importance on how we should be washed by the word of God.

Thy word is a lamp unto my feet, and a light unto my path. **(Psalms 119: 105) KJV**

The Table of Showbread

The Table of Showbread was located inside of the tabernacle. This part of the tabernacle was called the Holly Place. However, it represented the word of God.

The table of showbread was just what the title states that it was. It was actually a small table that was made out of Acacia wood and overlaid with gold. In addition, it consisted of twelve pieces on bread made out of fine flour. Therefore, the bread was placed on top of the table but were in rolls of six. There were six pieces of bread on one side and six pieces on the other. Likewise, the rolls were placed side by side of each other.

God also told Moses to place, dishes and bowls on top of the Table also.

The twelve pieces of bread that were on the table also had a symbolic meaning, it represented the twelve tribes of Israel and also Jesus Christ being the bread of life.

We mentioned Jacob had twelve sons that were born unto him. The names of the six sons that Leah bore for Jacob were as follows: Reuben, Simeon, Issachar, Zebulun, Levi and Juda.

Of course, Jesus Christ came from the tribe of Juda, and the Levites are the ones that God choose to serve in the tabernacle. **(Revelation 5:5) (Revelation 22:16) KJV**

Aaron, Moses, and Elizabeth were from the tribe of Levi. Elizabeth was the mother of John the Baptist and was also the cousin to Mary who was the mother to Jesus Christ.

Elizabeth was also the daughter of Aaron who was Moses brother. **(Luke 1: 34-36) KJV**

Leah had a sister named Rachael, and she bore Jacob two sons, and their names were Joseph and Benjamin. **(Geneses (30-22) KJV**

Jacob had four more son's by Leah's and Rachael's handmaidens. Their names were Dan, Napah, Gad and Asher.

Zilpah was Leah's handmaiden. She conceived and bore Jacob two sons. Their names were Gad and Asher. On the other hand, Rachel's handmaids name was Bilhah, and she bore Jacob two sons as well. The names of her sons were Dan and Naphtali.

Jacob asked Racheal's father if he could work seven years so that he could marry her. Laban agreed to allow him to marry her if he fulfilled his promise. But after the seven years had expired Laban tricked Jacob. Instead of telling him in the beginning that the first born had to be married, before the elder, he waited until afterwards, to let him know that this was a part of their culture. Consequently, Leah's father was a trickster because he wanted to use Jacob to work for him another seven years as well. This meant that he would have to wait fourteen years for the one that he really loved to be his wife. Of course, Jacob did not plain or anticipate for this to happen, but it did. But Jacob loved Racheal and had no intentions of marrying Leah. Since Leah was hated, God opened up her womb, but Rachel was barren. However, God allowed this to happen for his purpose.

Even, though Jacob loved Rachel, and she was more beautiful than Leah, the genealogy of Jesus Christ came through Leah's seed, and not Rachel. In addition, Jesus Christ was from the tribe of Juda, because Juda was one of Leah and Jacob's sons.

The Holy of Holies

The Holy of Holies was a place that only the high priest was allowed to enter, but they could only enter once a year. In addition, it could only take place on the Day of Atonement.

The Holy of Holies was a room that consisted of the Ark of the Covenant. This was the only piece of furniture that was in this particular room.

Which had the golden censer, and the ark of the covenant overlaid round about with gold, wherein was the golden pot that had manna, and Aaron's rod that budded, and the tables of the covenant. ***(Exodus 9:4)***

The Manna was the food that God had rained down from heaven when the Israelites were in the wilderness.

There was also a thick curtain that was placed between the Holy Place and the of Holies. These curtains were designed with Cherubim's which are angels.

Whether you know it or not satin was once a Cherubim that covered. I wonder whom did he cover?

Thou hast been in Eden the garden of God; every precious stone was thou covering, the sardius, topaz, and the diamond, the beryl, the onyx, and the jasper, the sapphire, the emerald, and the carbuncle, and gold: the workmanship of thy tabrets and thy pipes was prepared in thee in the day that thou wast created. Thou art anointed cherub that covereth; and I have set thee so: thou wast upon the holy mountain of God; thou hast walked up and down in the mist of the stones of fire. Thou was perfect in thou ways from the day that thou wast created, till iniquity was found in thee. **(Ezekiel 28:13-19) KJV**

    Therefore, because of his beauty satin became up- lifted, and iniquity was also found in him. Because of this God caste him down to the ground.
    I guess you'd like to know why did satin fall from grace ?
    Also, in heaven there are different types of angels that have different jobs. Michael is classified as an archangel, and one of his assignments is to protect Israel. In addition, each angel has different assignments just as humans that reside here on earth.

    Could it had been that these Cherubim's covered God, because he was so powerful? If you look at the pattern of the Mercy Seat there were Cherubim's that covered it as well. In addition, whenever the High priest would enter into the Holy of Holies the Lord's presence would show up between the Cherubim's and the Mercy Seat.
    The Day of Atonement was a day that the priest went into the Holy of Holies to offer sacrifices for himself and for the people. On the other hand, he had to prepare himself ahead of time so that he would not die while he was there.
    This is one reason that there were bells and pomegranates worn at the bottom of his robe just in case he would die, while doing his priestly duties.
    On the Day of Atonement, Aaron would cast lots to see which goat would be sacrificed for the sins of Israel, or which one would be set free.
    This goat would be called the scapegoat. The scapegoat would be the one that was set free and allowed to go into the wilderness. Likewise, this goat was used for the atonement for Israel's sins.
    The sins of the people would be transferred onto the scapegoat.
    The other goat had to be killed as a Burt offering as unto the Lord. Then Aaron would place the blood of the animal on the Mercy Seat which was located inside of the Holy of Holies. **(Leviticus16:6-29) KJV**

    Wherefore the law was our schoolmaster to bring us unto Christ, that we may be justified by faith. **(Galatians 3:24) KJV**

If you notice that the priest could not go into God's presence in a sinful state. He had to sanctify himself at least for the period of time that he was in the Holy of Holies.

Aaron which was Moses brother had four sons. There names were Eleazar, Ithamar, Nadab, and Abihu.

Nadab and Abihu decided that they would offer up to the Lord some strange fire, while they were in the tabernacle. Therefore, there went out fire from the Lord and consumed them. **(Leviticus 10) KJV**

Aaron and his sons were also high priest. They therefore, had to bring a young bull for a sin offering and a ram for as burnt offering for themselves as well. In addition, the presence of God would appear to them upon the mercy seat.

The young bull and the ram were the mediators for the sins of the people.

This story of Nadab and Abihu is symbolic of how we We must do things his way and not how's.

Nevertheless, not my will, but thine, be done. **(Luke22:42KJV)**

We want to make sure that God is pleased with our lives. Because there are two types of blessings. There are spiritual blessings and then there are natural blessings. Most of us are more concerned about the natural blessings which are temporal, but spiritual blessings are eternal. This is not saying that God does not want us to prosper. He's just saying don't focus on material things more than you do your soul.

But seek ye first the kingdom of God, and his righteousness; and all of these things shall be added unto you. **(Matthew 6: 33) KJV**

Most people are not aware that spiritual things must be revealed to us by the Spirit of God, but you must seek him for it most of the time.

But the natural man receiveth not the things of the Spirit of God: for they are foolishness unto him: neither can he know them, because they are spiritually discerned. But he that is spiritual judges all things, yet he himself is judged of no man. **(1st Corinthians 2:14-15) KJV**

What this is saying is that some things of God cannot be revealed to you until he opens your spiritual eyes. Until this takes place, we can only relate to our five senses. In other words, we are only in tune to what we see, hear, smell, feel and taste.

We are programmed into this natural realm as soon as we are born. One way that we are programed is through television, news, schools, colleges, movies, music, technology, people, family, and various experiences. But God will sometimes use people that we least expect to reveal himself to us.

God is sovereign, and he can do whatever he desires to do. He is all knowing, powerful, and is in control even when things are spiraling look out of control.

Therefore hath he mercy on whom he will have mercy, and whom he will he hardeneth. **(Romans 9:18)KJV**

But God hath chosen the foolish things of the world to confound the wise; and God hath chosen the weak things of the world to confound the things which are mighty; And base things of the world, and the things which are despised, hath God chosen, yea, and things which are not, to bring to nought things that are : That no flesh should glory in his presence. **(1st Corinthian 1:27-28)**

What this is saying is that God will take the weak, despised, and the rejects of this world and use them for his glory. The word confound means to confuse, stun, surprise, shake, and puzzle. Moreover, he said that no flesh should glory in his sight.

There is a continuous warfare going on no matter how close we are to God. Consequently, we can never get relaxed and think that we have arrived. We need to use every weapon that God has given us.

In Romans the seventh chapter the Apostle Paul spoke of the war that he had encountered in his flesh.

Even Apostle Paul had a war going on in his flesh, and he was one of the greatest Apostles that ever lived.

Paul once persecuted the people of God out of ignorance, but the Lord revealed himself to him as he was going to Damascus to put some of the saints in prison. On the other hand, this lets us know that all flesh is as grass and there is no good thing in it as well.

the inner man desires to please the Lord but your outer man is at war with it. Paul says in verse twenty-two that he delights in the law of God after the inner man.

The outer man is the man that we see in the mirror, but the inner man is the man that can't be seen.

This lets you know that we have an inner man and an outer man as well. But when I was in sin there was no war because I didn't know God and his ways. Most of the times I did whatever my flesh led me to do. Even though I had a conscious about certain things that I would do. Even when we don't know God, we still have an inner voice that sometimes lets us know that we are not doing what is right. On the other hand, even after you find God there will sometimes be a war going on inside of you, because the old man will try to come back alive if you allow it too.

For *the good that I would I do not: but the evil which I would not, that I do. Now if I do that I would not, it is no more I that do it, but sin that dwelleth in me. I find then a law, that, when I would do good, evil is present with me. For I delight in the law of God after the inward man: But I see another law in my members, warring against the law of my mind, and bringing me into captivity to the law of sin which is in my member. O wretched man that I am! who shall deliver me from the body of this death? I thank God through Jesus Christ our Lord. So with the mind I myself serve the law of God; but with the flesh the law of sin.*

Why do you think this was happing? *Paul goes on to say now if I do that I would not, it is no more I that do it, but sin that dwelleth in m.* **(Romans 7:14-25)KJV**

He stated that he delighted in in the law of God after the inward man. *But I see another law in my members, warring against the law of my mind, and bringing me into captivity to the law of sin which is in my members.*

Your members would be your eyes, mouth, hands, feet and etc.

Paul also stated that his body was the body of death, and in his flesh dwelt no good thing.

But he then goes on to say that I thank God through Jesus Christ our Lord. So that with the mind I myself serve the law of God; but with the flesh the law of sin.

In Romans the 8th chapter, *There is therefore now no condemnation to them which are in Christ Jesus, who walk not after the flesh, but after the Spirit.* **(Romans 8)KJV**

If you notice Paul is not just talking about just going to bible class and attending a church building. I'm not stating that we should not attend church, but Paul is talking about our bodies where God wants to dwell and use us for his services, because the actual church is a spiritual organism.

Consequently, Paul went on to say how the Mosaic Law was weak though the flesh, and how God sent his Son in the likeness of sinful flesh to condemn sin in the flesh. He says that the righteousness of God should be fulfilled in us that walk not after the flesh but after the Spirit.

For to be carnally minded is death; but to be spiritually minded is life and peace. In other words, the mind is the powerhouse for the entire body.

Because the carnal mind is enmity against God: for it is not subject to the law of God, neither indeed can be.

So then they that are in the flesh cannot please God. But ye are not in the flesh, but in the Spirit, if so be that the Spirit of God dwell in you. Now if any man have not the Spirit of Christ, he is none of his. **(Romans 8:1-16)KJV**

I guess you wonder what does the word carnal means? The definition for this word carnal would be sensual, sexual appetite, temporal, worldly and indulgence.

This scripture talks about the mind, because the mind is the powerhouse for the body. *Let this mind be in you, which was also in Christ Jesus: Who, being in the form of God, thought it not robbery to be equal with God.* **(Philippians 2:5) KJV**

One of the powerful or strong holds that people have to deal with is sexual sins.

Now concerning the things whereof ye wrote unto me: it is good for a man to not touch a woman. Nevertheless, to avoid fornication, let every man have his own wife, and let every woman have her own husband. **(1ST Corinthians 7:2)KJV**

Paul was writing to the Corinthian church because some of them were fornicating or committing sexual acts and doing other ungodly things.

However, once you open up the door to fleshly desires it's sometimes hard to close.

Under the Mosaic law if a person was caught fornicating or committing adultery they would be stoned to death. Consequently, we should thank God for his grace and mercy in these last and evil days.

The reason that there were so many virgins at that particular time, is because sexual sins were not tolerated. But this a different generation from what it was in the past. Also, the young ladies married at a very young age. However, this could had been the reason that they married so young so that they could keep the commandments of the Lord.

Furthermore, this lets us know that sexual sins are very dangerous in the spiritual realm, especially if you are filled with the Spirit of God. This could also be a doorway for spirits to come back into the temple that they once occupied. However, there are people that are more susceptible to spirits than other. In addition, when you sleep with someone you sometimes may feel like you are one with that person. You may also feel as if you can't live without them.

There are some people that may not ever experience ever feeling like this way. Why? Because they may have another type of spirit. It could be that they don't desire a committed relationship and will not allow themselves to be attached to one person. Therefore, they could have a sexual demon that can't be satisfied. They may have picked up the spirit of lust and may not be able to control themselves. Then there are some people that may not be aware of what is happening to them, especially if they don't believe in the unseen world. **(1stCorinthians 6:16) KJV**

Moreover, your body was not made for fornication but, was made for the Lord. Likewise, it was made for him to use as a vessel and for this glory.

*Stolen waters are sweet, and bread eaten in secret is pleasant. But he knoweth not that the dead are there; and that her guest are in the depths of hell. On the other hand, the bible talks about virtuous woman who can find? **(Proverbs 31:10-31) KJV***

What is the meaning of the word virtuous? It is a woman that has high morals, honorable, righteous, and upright as well.

Who can find a virtuous woman? for her price is far above rubies. The heart of her husband doth safely trust in her, so that he shall have no need of spoil. She will do him good and not evil all the days of her life. She seeketh wool, and flax, and worketh willingly with her hands. She is like the merchants' ships; she bringeth her food from afar. She riseth also while it is yet night, and giveth meat to her household, and a portion to her maidens. She considereth a field, and buyeth it: with the fruit of her hands she planteth a vineyard. She girdeth her loins with strength, and strengtheneth her arms. She perceiveth that her merchandise is wisdom; and in her tongue is the law of kindness. She looketh well to the ways of her household, and eateth not the bread of idleness. He children arise up, and call her blessed; her husband also, and he praiseth her. Many daughters have done virtuously, but thou excellest them all. Favour is deceitful, and beauty is good: her candle goeth not out by night. She layeth her hands to the spindle, and her hands hold the distaff. She stretcheth out her hand to the poor; yea, she reacheth forth her hands to the needy. She is not afraid of the snow for her household: for all her household are clothed with scarlet. She maketh herself coverings of tapestry; her clothing is silk and purple. Her husband is known in the gates, when he sitteth among the elders of the land. She maketh fine linen, and selleth it; and delivereth girdles into the merchant. Strength and honour are her clothing; and she shall rejoice in time to come. She openeth her mouth with vain: but a woman that feareth the Lord, she shall be praised. Give her of the fruit of her hands; and let her own works praise her in the gates.

Chapter 3

Understanding the Mosaic Law

The bible speaks of many laws and various kinds of them under the Mosaic Law and there were 613 of them that the Israelites had to follow. Some of them were as follows:

Deuteronomy 19th chapter this chapter talks about under the law it states that if a person killed someone unintentionally that there were cities of refuge for them to flee to for safety. These cities existed because family member of the deceased would sometimes seek revenge.

Likewise, these cities were called the cities of refuge.

These six cities were given to the Levites that worked in the temple, because none of the other tribes were allowed to work in it.

In the book of numbers, it also mentions these six cities as well. On the other hand, the innocent person could not leave the city until he stood before the congregation and they had to wait the death of the high priest as well. If he decided to leave before it was time and thy were killed by the diseased family member, they would not be found guilty of murder.

This reminds me of what can happen if we are not covered under the blood of Jesus or if we leave from under his protection.

You can use these cities of refuge as symbolic for our lives as well. It reminds me of when you purchase insurance in the natural. When you have insurance, it covers you if anything goes wrong.

For we wrestle not against flesh and blood, but against principalities, against powers, against the rulers of the darkness of this world, against spiritual wickedness in high places. ***(Ephesians 6:12) KJV***

In 2nd Corinthians 4:4 it mentions that satin is the god of this world. This just means that he is the god of this worldly system. If you notice I didn't capitalize his name on purpose, because he likes for us to give him the glory.

Another Law that was under the Mosaic Law is if a person was found slain in a field and no one knew who had killed that them, then the elders and judges were to measure the city that was next to the slain person. In addition, the judges had to take heifer, which is a young cow that never gave birth, and that had never been wrought with or had not drawn the yoke.

The word wrought means that the animal had never been used for work, and the word yoke is a wooden crosspiece that is placed over the neck of two animals and is used to pull a cart as well.

First, if a person was found slain in a field, and if no one knew who had committed that particular crime the elders and judges had to come forth and measure the cities that was around the slain person. Second, the priest had to prove that he didn't know anything about the crime that was committed. Third the elders that lived in that city would have to take a heifer which is a young cow that had never been used for work, and bring it to a valley, that had not been plowed or planted. In addition, it had to be running water in that particular valley. The priest which were the sons of Levi that ministered unto the Lord would come and hear the controversy of the case. Finally, the elders of that city where the slain person had been slain would come and wash their hands over the heifer and thy would cut off the head of the animal.

Then they shall answer and say, our hands have not shed this blood, neither have our eyes seen it. **(Deuteronomy 21) KJV**

This is showing you how God hates sin and cannot tolerate it in his presence. The scripture tells us that Jesus is on the right hand of the Father and is making intercessions for the saints of God, and we therefore do not need these animal sacrifices any longer. He also is our high priest and is a perfect sacrifice for our sins as well. Even though we have to do our part. **(Hebrew 9:11- 28)**

Remember we stated that the Mosaic Law was our master to bring us unto Christ, and it was a pattern of what was to come. It was a temporarily fix for a fallen world. **(Galatians 3:24) KJV**

Everything, that was placed in the temple was a symbolic symbol for salvation that is under grace. Under the Mosaic Law you could be saved by works alone, because Jesus had not come at that particular time.

This is one reason that the thief on the cross could be saved when he was being crucified along with Jesus, because he was still under the Mosaic Law.

There were two malefactors on the cross when Jesus was crucified. What is a malefactor? Well, a malefactor is criminal or someone that breaks the law.

One of the malefactors asked Jesus to remember him when he comes into his Kingdom.

And Jesus said unto him, Verily, I say unto thee, Today shalt thou be with me in paradise. **(Luke 23: 32- 43) KJV**

Rules for the Priest Under the Mosaic Law

The priest had to reference God while they were in the sanctuary or they would die This is also symbolic for how we should respect and reference God and his presence at all times. However, In the Old Testament if anyone showed disrespect to God, while they were in the temple thy would drop dead immediately. But under grace you don't drop dead immediately it will just catch up with you in the end. Even though they can still repent while there is time.

Because sentence against an evil work is not executed speedily, therefore the heart of the sons of men is fully set in them to do evil. **(Ecclesiastics 8:11) KJV**

You notice in the verse it uses the word speedily meaning, because judgment does not take place right away, people sometimes will harden their hearts towards God. Therefore, this can cause them to become more comfortable in their sins, and in their minds they may believe that they have gotten away with their evil deeds.

Even though the Lord may still be blessing them in the natural, it does not necessarily mean that God is pleased with their lives. But because they are being blessed naturally, they may take it as a sign that they are pleasing to the Father. God also reigns on the just as well as the unjust.

However, a lot of things that we suffer in this life could be because of the choices that we may have made. Most of the times we don't want to admit to ourselves, that this could be the reason why we are going through the things that God never intended for us to suffer. In addition, the wicked may receive more temporal blessings and the righteous more spiritual blessings.

Even though God is very merciful, he does have another side that most people hesitate to talk about. I know that we are not perfect, and we all fall short of the glory of God. But there is a such thing as crossing the line.

The priest had to wash their hands and feet before entering the tabernacle or they would die. This is symbolic for how God hates sin. **(Exodus 30:17)KJV**

For the word of God is quick, and powerful, and sharper than any two twoedged sword, piercing even to the dividing asunder of soul and spirit, and of the joints and marrow, and is a discerner of the thoughts and intents of the heart. Neither is there any creature that is not manifest in his sight: but all things are naked and opened unto the eyes of him with whom we have to do. **(Hebrews 4:12-14) KJV**

This is stating that nothing is hid from God and all things are open unto him as well.

Whither shall I go from thy Spirit? Or whither shall I flee from thy presence? If I ascend up into heaven, thou art there: if I make my bed in hell, behold thou art there. If I take the wings of the morning, and dwell in the uttermost parts of the sea; Even there shall thy hand lead me, and thy right hand shall hold me.

This is a psalm that David had written, while going through life's journey. **(Psalms 139: 7-12) KJV**

If you think of a two-edged sword when it Pierces the body, it does not feel good. The word sometimes will uncover our sins so that we can face ourselves and repent. We may be trying to run but there is no hiding place.

Have you ever had a dream or spoke to someone and they said something relating to what you were going through at that particular time? You knew that it had to come from the Lord, because they didn't know your circumstances, and you may not have ever met this person before. You also knew that it was a word for only you? You may have needed an answer to something or could had been doing things that were not pleasing in Gods sight.

This is because his word is like a two-edged sword and is a revealer of the intents of the heart.

The heart is deceitful above all things, and desperately wicked: who can know it? **(Jeramiah 17:9) KJV**

I guess some people would like to know what is the meaning of the word repentance?

We were all born in sin and shapen in iniquity. This means we were born in the state of sin.

The wicked are estranged from the womb: they go astray as soon as they are born, speaking lies. **(Palms 58)KJ**

We were all born with an Adamic nature. Why? Because of what Adam and Eve did in the garden of Eden. Thereby, they disobeyed the commandment that God had given them. In addition, when they committed this particular sin in the Garden of Eden, they took on a new nature. Likewise, they took on an Adamic nature.

There is one thing that we should be striving for and that is to not leave the world in the state that we were born in, but we want to leave the world hid in God until these calamities pass. Even though we will never be perfect, but we want to be transformed by the power of God day by day.

Some people are now saying that everyone sins. But there is a difference between practicing sin and committing a sin. If that was the case, then there would be no difference in the way we were before God transforms us. In other words, you would be the same as you were before you knew him.

Lord I know I've been changed. We are to allow God to perfect us unto his into his image. We want to be transformed to be like our Father which is in heaven.

In order for you to get to know God the way that you should you will have to be tried in the fire.

Even after you find him, he will still be molding and making you. Therefore, he must continue to work on you like a potter does with his clay.

You will sometimes wonder why things in your life are getting worst instead of better. There may be times in your life situations may seem to intensify as well. This sometimes takes place, because satin knows that he is losing ground. Even though your inner man may be growing, there are times that things from the outside may seem to get worst. satin also can make problems appear to be worst then they really are. Now do you see why this is called a warfare?

Sometimes he will use the people that you love the most to discourage you as well. This is an example of what happens in a natural fight. The person hits you in the place that it hurts the most.

Many are the afflictions of the righteous: but the Lord delivereth him out of them all. (psalms 34:19)KJV

My little children, these things write I unto you, that ye sin not, And if any man sin, we have an advocate with the Father, Jesus Christ the righteous: And he is the propitiation for our sins: and not for ours only, but also for the sins of the whole world. And hereby we do know that we know him, if we keep his commandments. He that saith, I know him, and keepeth not his commandments, is a liar, and the truth is not in him. (John 2:1) KJV

Because the Lord knew that we would falter at times was the reason that this scripture was written. I guess you say why do we falter? We falter sometimes, because the flesh is weak, and we have a sinful nature that is at war with our new nature as well.

It may take some time for God to perfect you, but you should be changing into a better person as time goes on.

Wherefore, as by one man sin entered into the world, and death by sin; and so death passed upon all men, for that all have sinned.

For as by one man's disobedience many were made sinners, so by the obedience of one shall many be made righteous. (Romans 5:19) KJV

This is saying when Adam and Eve sinned, they placed everyone that was born under condemnation. Moreover, when we are born again from above then we will go back to the original state that we were in before this took place.

Furthermore, remember in the Old Testament they brought burnt offerings for their sins. I guess you wonder what sin did the burnt offering represent? This particular offering represented the state of sin that the person was born in. In other words, this is why the entire animal had to be consumed on the Bronze Alter and could not be eaten. In addition, this was not the only sin that this offering was used for.

There are times that it can be very difficult for someone to see that they are sinners, because they may have a good nature. I once had a friend tell me that it was hard for her to get saved, because she didn't do that much wrong. This is why God sometimes allow our world to be turned upside down, so that we can see the need for salvation, and turn from our wicked ways.

God will turn the heat up and may allow you to go through something that no man nor you will be able to bring yourself out of. Therefore, you will need a supernatural experience for this one.

I'm not stating that this works for everyone, because man has a free will and can reject the call of God. Moreover, some of our sins may be hidden and may not be as noticeable to people.

We often think of drinking, smoking, fornicating and cheating as the worst sins. But the hidden sins could be gossiping, self-righteousness, holding grudges, love of money, fear, unbelief, pride, high minded and the cares of this world.

Someone that drinks, smoke, and fornicate could have a better heart then someone that may not indulge any of these things.

There are some people that will hurt themselves but would never hurt another person intentionally.

This is why the bible says that man looks on the outer appearance, but God looks at the heart.

On the other side of the coin all is sin, and God hates all of it. People say sin is sin and it is, but there are some sins that may have a stronger hold on a person in the spiritual realm. In other words, it is called having a strong hold, because we are not fighting flesh and blood but principalities. Also, there are some sins that can open the door to other demons and make the person worst then they were before. **(Luke 11:24-26)kJV**

If you study your bible you will see that God used words such as sins, abomination, and trespasses. Even though it is all classified as sin.

In the Old Testament you will notice that they brought certain animals for certain sins.

A person that practiced witchcraft or homosexuality would be an example of a sin of abomination. Both of these practices could have a strong hold on a person, and it is against nature as well. This is why there is a difference in a person that may be a liar or a fornicater, then someone that may indulge in witchcraft. On the other hand, it is still all sin and you can still be lost if you die in in that state.

The meaning of the word abomination would be something that is rotten or stinks in Gods nostrils. On the other hand, the meaning of the word sin would be to miss the mark or fall short.

Also, a wicked person is worst then a person that is a sinner. Because, a wicked person is someone that has no moral standards nor has no conscious. **(Romans 1:18-32**

David missed the mark when he slept with Bathsheba and then impregnated her but he was not classified as wicked. He attempted to get her husband Uriah to sleep with her to make him believe that the child had been conceived by him. But God did not allow this to happen. Therefore, David became fearful and told Joel to put Uriah on the front line of the army, so that his chances of being killed would be greater. As you can see this is an example how one sin could led to another. **(2nd Samuel 12:1-24)**

Jesus answered, Verily, verily, I say unto thee, Except a man be born of water and of the Spirit, he cannot enter into the kingdom of God. *(John 3:5) KJV*

Even after you repent this does not mean that you will not make mistakes, because God will still be working on you like a piece of clay, but the difference is that when you do make a mistake you will not feel comfortable, about it as you did in the past.

Repentance should become a way of life for all of us, because we are in a war but not with flesh and blood. But we're fighting principalities and rulers of the darkness of this world. Therefore, when your being constantly attacked it could be that you are getting closer to your breakthrough. You must take your blessing by force.

And from the days of John the Baptize until now the kingdom of heaven suffereth violence, and the violent take it by force. (**Matthew 11:12**)

This is saying that you must sometimes fight for what you want from God, but he didn't say that it would be easy. However, we sometimes fight for success in the natural world but do not but the same energy into our spirit man which will last throughout eternity.

There are scriptures that people are quoting incorrectly and without understanding. People are saying you can't judge them. This scripture is in the bible, but if you don't rightly divide the word you may not be able to comprehend what this verse is actually saying. In addition, the reason that people are quoting this is because someone from the world started this saying. Most people don't know that there are different types of judgments written in the bible. Let's see what the bible has to say about it.

Moreover, if we cannot judge, then why do the same people that make these statements get upset when someone mistreat them, or say something that offends them? If that was the case, then if someone did a serious crime against one of their family members then that should mean that they should not be judged as well. They should just say I can't judge that person and move on with their lives. It would be good if we were strong enough to do that of course. But if you are going to use this scripture then you have to use It across the board.

There are different types of judgments that is written in the bible. This is what is quoted in the scripture

Judge not according to the appearance but judge righteous judgement. **(John 7;24)** *KJV*

But this is for the saints that are walking up rightly in Gods sight. This is saying that we should not judge things by appearances only. This is not an easy thing to do because we are programmed and have been doing this our entire lives.

This is why you should ask the Lord to increase your discernment, so that you will not be deceived by appearances. Furthermore, even if you don't know the Lord you still have a certain amount of discernment, even though there are different levels of it. Some people may have more of it than others.

There are two types of discernment one is natural, and the other is spiritual. When you have spiritual discernment, you're able to see what others are not able to in the spiritual realm.

Even animals have a certain amount discernment. Have you ever watched the news, and seen when some animals sensed danger they would, therefore move to a higher ground?

These instincts come from the Lord. What a mighty God we serve.

But strong meat belongeth to them that are of full age, even those who by reason of use have their senses exercised to discern both good and evil. **(Hebrews 5:14)** *KJV*

For the Lord seeth not as man seeth; for man looketh on the outward appearance, but the Lord looketh on the heart. **(1st Samuel 16)** *KJV*

For if we would judge ourselves, we should not be judged.
But when we are judged, we are chastened of the Lord, that we should not be condemned with the world. **(1st Corinthians 11:31-32)** *KJV*

The judgement that this scripture is speaking of is called the Great White Throne Judgement.

This is saying that we should take inventory of ourselves so that we won't be judged with the world. Sometimes we can see the mote in someone else's eye but not our own.

The second death means that a person died in sin and will be separated from God throughout eternity

And death and hell were cast into the lake of fire. This is the second death. ***(Revelation 20:14) KJV***

Judge not, that ye be not judged. For with what judgement ye judge, ye shall be judged: and with *what measure ye mete, it shall be measured to you again.*

And why beholdest thou the mote that is in thy brother's eye, but considerest not the beam that is in thine own eye? ***(Matthew 7:1-5) KJV***

You have to read the entire chapter to get an understanding to why this was written in the first place. This scripture is talking about someone that is judging another person, but their lives are not much better. If you continue to read the entire chapter you will see that God also called them hypocrites.

Another reason that Paul was speaking in this manner is because in 1st Corinthians 6:2, some of the saints had returned back into some of their old sinful ways, which God had delivered them from. if you take the time to read the entire chapter you will get a better understanding of why Paul was speaking in this manner. You just can't take one scripture from the bible, and not read the entire chapter for a complete understanding of why it was being said.

These scriptures were written, because the saints in the Corinthian church had taken each other to court for various things. Paul was telling them that they should not be go before the unbelievers to settle their problems, because they would be judging angels in the future, and if they were qualified to judge angels then they should be able to judge things in this life also.

Dare any of you, having a matter against another, go to law before the unjust, and not before the saints?

Do ye not know that the saints shall judge the world? and if the world shall be judged by you, are ye unworthy to judge the smallest matters?

Know ye not that we shall judge angels? how much more things that pertain to this life?

If then ye have judgments of things pertaining to this life, set them to judge who are least esteemed in the church.

I speak to your shame. Is it so, that there is not a wise man among you? no, not one that shall be able to judge between his brethren?

But brotheren goeth to law with brother, and that before the unbelievers.

Now therefore there is utterly a fault among you, because ye go to law one with another. Why do ye not rather take wrong? why do ye not rather suffer yourselves to be defrauded ? **(1ˢᵗ Corinthians 6:1-16) KJV**

Also, he mentioned to them that the saints will be judged for their works as well. But they will not be judged in the Great White Throne judgement, because this judgement is for the wicked dead, and those whose names were not found written in the book of life.

An example, of works that a saint may be rewarded for would be like the friend that brought me to the Lord. Therefore, when I get to heaven she will be rewarded because I kept the faith. **(1ˢᵗ Corinthians 3:11**20**) KJV**

I hope that you can see that pattern of how sometimes things in our natural world are also similar to the things in the spiritual realm.

If you read with an understanding, it lets you know that you must be holy for the Spirit of God to dwell in you. This does not mean that he is not with you before you are filled. The Lord will sanctify you before he fills you with his Spirit as well. On the other hand, he may start dealing with you, but you may not understand why your life is being turned upside down. However, the Lords chastens those that he loves.

Let me explain something else to you when I say that you must be holy for God to dwell in you. I hope that you don't think that I'm saying that you have to be perfect. If that was the case, then no one would be saved. It just means that you have to be in right standing with God and continue to allow him to keep making and molding you. You must also surrender yourself totally to him. This may not be an thing easy thing to do at first, but with Christ you can do all things.

Another secret to seeking the Lord is that you must hunger and thirst after righteousness, because this will motivate you into finding him. When you seek him with your whole heart then you will find him.

Furthermore, John the Baptize was the only human being that was born with the Holy Ghost. If that is the case, then how do you receive I it guess you say? Do you just join a local church, or is there more to it? We will discuss this more in dept in in this book.**(Luke 1:5:15)**K

Know ye not that ye are the temple of God, and that the Spirit of God dwelleth in you? If any man defile the temple of God, him shall God destroy; for the temple of God is holy, which temple ye are. **(1ˢᵗ Corinthians 3:16)KJV**

He used the word temple in this sentence for a reason. Remember in the Old Testament the temple was portable, and it could only move when the cloud moved, which was God's presence. But after Jesus died on the cross our bodies are now the temple that God desires to use for his glory.

Chapter 4

Why You Should to be Baptized in the Name of the Lord Jesus Christ

What does it mean to be born of the water? John the Baptize was the only human being that was born with the Holy Ghost. One of the reasons that he was so special was, because he had to baptize our Lord and savior Jesus Christ.

John the Baptize mother's name was Elizabeth and his father's name were Zacharia. Zacharia was a priest that worked in the temple. This means that Zacharia had to have been a Levite, because you couldn't work in the temple unless you were from that particular tribe. This was one of the reasons that God mentioned that John the Baptize was the greatest among women and he was commanded not to drink wine nor strong drink.

The name of the angel that visited Zacharia while he was ministering in the temple was Gabriel. He was told by the angel to name the child John and that he should not drink strong drink or wine as well. **(Luke 1:13-15**

However, you may not be aware that Mary, which was the mother of Jesus was the cousin of Elizabeth as well. In addition, Mary the mother of Jesus had the same encounter with Gabriel, almost at the same time. Because Jesus and John were only six months' apart.

Mary and Elizabeth both began to praise their God for what he had done in their lives. But while they were praising him John leaped in Elizbeth's belly and she was filled with the Holy Ghost. **(Luke 1-26-42) KJV**

I guess you're asking how Elizabeth could receive the Holy Ghost if Jesus hadn't died on the cross as of yet. This could take place because she had conceived a child born with the Holy Ghost. In other words, this would not be an ordinary child. But on the other hand, Mary didn't receive the Holy Ghost on the same day that Elizabeth did. God does things at his own timing.

As you can see, the Lord is dealing with only the seed of Abraham, Isaac and Jacob to accomplish his plan.

In the scriptures it mentions that when Mary came to visit Elizabeth, they both testified to the visitation of the angel named Gabriel. **(Luke 1:26) KJV)**

Let's talk about the importance of baptism. The bible speaks of two baptisms in the bible.

John answered, saying unto them all, I indeed baptize you with water; but one mightier than I cometh, the latchet of whose shoes I am not worthy to unloose: he shall baptize you with the Holy Ghost and with fire. **(Luke 3:16) KJV**

Jesus often used natural things to compare with spiritual things. And if we were to study some of these things it would help us to learn more about life in general.

Romans 6:6 What shall we say then? Shall we continue in sin, that grace may abound? God forbid. How shall we, that are dead to sin, live any longer therein? Know ye not, that so many of us as were baptized into Jesus Christ were baptized into his death? Therefore we are buried with him by baptism unto his death: that like as Christ was raised up from the dead by the glory of the Father, even so we also should walk in the newness of life. For if we have been planted together in his likeness of his death, we shall be also in the likeness of his resurrection.

Knowing this, that our old man is crucified with him, that the body of sin might be destroyed, that henceforth we should not serve sin.

What this scripture is saying is just because God is merciful gives us no right to trample over his grace and mercy.

It is also saying that we should not serve sin. This means that we should not practice sin, even though we are not perfect and may fall short at times. This just means that you won't practice sin the way that you did before founding the Lord. But we are aware that people do sometimes get weak in the flesh. This is why we need our spirits refreshed on a contiguous basis. However, his grace is sufficient, and he is well able to keep us from falling. You also may have grown in one area of your life, but God could be still working on you in other areas as well.

If you noticed I used the word sometimes when it comes to our flesh getting weak. The reason that I said this is, because sin will not be a way of life for you after you've changed into the new creature that God has created, nor will you practice sin the way that you once did in the past.

Therefore, we know that when a person Is buried in the natural world that their entire body goes into the ground. However, in the spiritual realm the same should occur as well. Moreover, the old man should be left in the water and the new man should be emerging after this wonderful experience.

If you think about it even Jesus was baptized by his cousin John, the Baptize. This lets us know that we must be buried with the Father in order to be resurrected with him, when he comes back for us. This is one of the ways that we are identified with him. Moreover, if you haven't repented of your sins it just means that you just went through a formality and it was a waste of your time.

There will be churches that will not explain this to you, because some of them are only interested in filling up their seats on Sunday mornings. On the other hand, some of them are only telling you what they know and may mean well in their hearts. In addition, because we have a sinful nature we sometimes like these kinds of churches, because we don't have to change.

Furthermore, our flesh should be dying daily from the things of this world. But in order for this to take place you must repent of your sins, otherwise this will not work for you. In order for us to be identified with the Lord Jesus Christ, we must follow his example as well. Moreover, we must be partakers of his death, burial, and resurrection in order to be identified with him when he returns. Furthermore, we must take on his name which is the lord Jesus Christ because we are going to be his new bride. And we must sanctify our temples so that he can come and dwell with us forever.

The Lord desires to use us for his glory. He wants to use our eyes, hands, feet, and what's us to be lights of the world, because the world is in gross darkness, and needs a light. For these are surely perilous times that we are living in. Even though some of us may be prospering in the natural this has nothing to do with what I'm talking about. The word says that

For when they shall say, peace and safety; then sudden destruction cometh upon them as travail upon a women with child; and they shall not escape. (1ˢᵗThessalonians 5:3)KJV

If a plant is planted incorrectly it will eventually die. On the other hand, you must follow the directions that is on the package if you want good results. Therefore, you can't do it your way and then expect the plant to survive. Therefore, we must also follow the instructions that was given to us by our Lord and savior Jesus Christ and continue to crucify the works of the flesh.

Neither is there salvation in any other: for there is none other name under heaven given among men, whereby we must be saved. **(Acts 4: 12) KJV**

And whatsoever ye do in word or deed, do all in the name of the Lord Jesus, giving thanks to God and the Father by him. **(Colossians 3:17) KJV**

The definition of the word deed would be an act or something that is done.

Whenever someone repents and is baptized in the name of the Lord Jesus Christ, they have taken on their husband's new name because we are his future bride.

I guess some people are asking why does the scripture say in Matthew go ye baptizing in the name of the Father and of the Son and of the Holy Ghost?

An example of this would be when a man marries a woman, she takes on his last name but not his titles. He could be a preacher, counselor, husband, and someone's uncle but this is not his name. This is similar to how it is in the spiritual realm.

In order for us to be identified with our husband which is the Lord Jesus Christ, we must take on his full name.

The key word here is identified. What this is saying is that when he looks at us, he must see himself. In other words, we must have his DNA.

Baptism also gives us as a good conscience toward God as well. **(1ˢᵗ Peter 3:21) KJV**

Paul had gone to the city to Ephesus, and while he was there, he encountered certain disciples that were believers, but they had not received the Holy Ghost. Therefore, he asked them had they received the Holy Ghost since they had believed. They stated that they had never heard of it before.

And he said unto them, unto what then were ye baptized? And they said, unto John's baptism.

Paul explained to them that John's baptism was for repentance to get them ready for the one that would come after him.

When they heard this, they were baptized in the name of the Lord Jesus. And when Paul had laid his hands on them, the Holy Ghost came on them; and they spake with tongues, and prophesied. And all the men were about twelve. (Acts: 19:1-7) KJV

If you notice they were all baptized the second time for a reason, because John's baptism was just temporal. This is what is called being born of the water, but you must repent first. Otherwise you just have a form of Godliness. They also needed to receive both baptisms. One that consisted of being baptized in water and the other baptism which is of the Spirit. **(Acts 19)KJV**

However, we must be born of the water and the Spirit because flesh and blood cannot enter into the kingdom of God. Furthermore, if any man has not his Spirit, he is none of his.

Also, in Acts the 8th chapter it mentions about the persecution on the church that was located in Jerusalem. This story took place during the time that Saul whose name was changed to Paul was persecuting the saints of God. There was another saint whose name was Stephen that was a martyr. He was stoned to death because of his belief in Jesus Christ. Furthermore, the saints were scattered abroad because they were being persecuted. The bible states that

And we know that all things work together for good to them that love God, to them who are the called according to his purpose. **(Romans 8:28) KJV**

On the other hand, this still worked out for the good of the church, because Phillip went to the city of Samaria and witnessed to the people that did not know about the Lord. In addition, there were people that were demon possessed and had palsy. Others were also healed from various diseases as well. And there was great joy in that city.

Prayer was made for the people to receive the Holy Ghost. In other words, some of them had been baptized but had not received it as of yet.

In Acts chapter 8:14 it mentions about the Apostles that were at Jerusalem. They had heard that the people in Samaria had received the word of God. Therefore, they sent for Peter and John to minister unto them, so that they would receive the Holy Ghost. The reason that this was done is because the Holy Ghost had not fallen on them that were not baptized. But it had fallen on them that had been.

Then laid they their hands on them, and they received the Holy Ghost. **(Acts 8:14-24) KJV**

Moreover, in the book of Acts you will notice that the disciples, Mary the mother of Jesus, and his brothers were in the upper room when the Holy Ghost fell on the day of Pentecost. Even Mary the mother of Jesus had to be born again of the Spirit. **(Acts 1:1-15) KJV**

In addition, Mary was born under the Mosaic Law, and Jesus had to die for her as well in order to bring about a new covenant. Jesus was reaching many people and their lives were changing as well. This was one of the main reasons that the Romans and some of the Jews rejected Jesus because he was breaking a lot of the laws that they were supposed to be abiding by under the Mosaic law. Consequently, he was going against their system and customs. Some of them rejected him out of ignorance as well. This is why he stated on the cross when he was being crucified Father forgive them for, they know not what they do.

They did not know who Jesus was in biblical days, nor do they know who we are as well.

Thank it not strange If you are persecuted for righteousness sake because you are his child and sometimes this may prove that you are identified with him as well. And the scripture mentions

Should Jesus bear the cross alone and all the world go free. Yes, there's a cross for everyone and theirs's a across for me. Whereby, this is another sign that we are identified with our Lord and Savior Jesus Christ.

*Marvel not, my brethren, if the world hates you.***1st John 3:12**

But the Lord was tired of the people bringing, bulls' doves and animal sacrifices to the temple every day. Remember, we stated that there were 613 laws that the Israelites had to abide by, and it was not just the ten commandment that were given to Moses on Mount Sani, but there were additional laws that most people don't know about in these modern days. On the other hand, the Israelites would bring their sacrifices every day to the temple but would return to doing the same sins as before. Moreover, Jesus Christ was our perfect sacrifice and only had to die for our sins once.

We, therefore, don't have to go to a priest to confess our sins, because he was born in sin the same way you and I. Which means that he was born with an Adamic nature as well. If Mary had to be born again what about you and I. Jesus Christ came on earth for us to have the victory over the world, the flesh, and the devil.

God is a Spirit: and thy that worship him must worship in Spirit and in truth. **(John 4:24) KJV**

Consequently, if we do happen to fall or falter, we have an advocate with the Father Jesus Christ the righteous. Therefore, we can also go to him, because we now have a high priest that can be touched by the feelings of our infirmities as well.

How is it that we have an advocate with the Father? First, God wrapped himself in a body and came down in the likeness of sinful flesh? There is a reason why he did this for us. One reason that he came down in the likeness of sinful flesh is, so that he could identify with what humans go through on a daily basis.

The second reason, that he came in the likeness of sinful flesh is so that he could defeat the world, the flesh and the devil.

Would you believe that after Jesus was crucified that he went down into hell and preached to the souls that were in prison?

Some of the souls that he preached to, were some of the same people that was disobedient during the times of Noah, and they had been warned that it was going to rain for forty days and forty nights. **(1ˢᵗ peter 3: 18-20) KJV**

There is nothing new under the sun, because the same thing is going on in the times that we are living in as well.

On the other hand, we will have no excuse on judgement day, because Jesus was rejected, persecuted, abused, tempted, hated, and crucifies as well. Would you believe that Jesus's was rejected by some of his family members as well? Because even his four brothers didn't believe in him. **(Mark 6)**

Beloved, thank it not strange concerning the fiery which is to try you, as though some strange thing happened unto you. **(*1ˢᵗPeter 12: 1) KJV*

Chapter 5

What is Sanctification?

I know that this subject will not be very popular for what I am about to say, but God does not change even though the times may have. Moreover, if you don't plan to sanctify yourself, and yield yourself to God and allow him to mold and make you, then you will most likely remain the same.

When you become hungry for God and seek him with your whole heart, then you will find him. This is why God sometimes allows the enemy to shake our world, because he loves us, and he chasten those whom he loves as well. But you must remember that the local church is where we go to feed our spirits, and to get away from the cares of this life. Moreover, every church is not necessarily the house of God.

I can remember going to a church with one of my coworkers, and the pastor of the church was his family member. But I really didn't get anything out of the service that day. On the other hand, after leaving this particular church my spirit felt very bound. My, spirit knew that something was not right about this church. It took me an entire week to get my spirit Intune with God, like it had been before.

What made this situation so bad is that about the same time my niece had died, and I had to sing a solo at her funeral, but I was having a hard time feeling God's presence while I was singing.

Not forsaking the assembling of ourselves together, as the manner of some is; but exhorting one another: and so much the more, as ye see the day approaching. **(Hebrews 10:25) KJV**

Let me make this plain, I'm not saying that we don't need the local church because we do. An example of the local church would be like your car. If you don't take care of your car it will not run properly, and eventually it will break down. Therefore, your temple which is your spirit needs to be fed the same way that your body needs to be fed.

So, then faith cometh by hearing, and hearing by the word of God. **(Romans 10:17) KJV**

You will not find a perfect church here on earth. Why? Because the local assembly is not the actual church, but our bodies are the temple that God wants to dwell in. And even after God has revealed himself to us, we sometimes may not summit ourselves totally to him.

Consequently, walking with God is personal for each and every one of us. Of course, there is such a thing as crossing the line when It comes to leaving or joining a church

Jesus taught the disciples many parables. What is a parable? A parable is a simple story, that teaches you a moral or something that is spiritual.

Another parable put he forth unto them, saying, The kingdom of heaven is likened unto a man which sowed good seed in his field: But while men slept, his enemy came and sowed tares among the wheat, and went his way. But when the blade was sprung up, and brought forth fruit, then appeared the tares also. So the servants of the household came and said unto him, Sir, didst not thou sow good seed unto thy field? from whence then hath it tears? He said unto them, An enemy hath done this. The servants said unto him, wilt thou then that we go and gather them up? But he said, Nay; lest while ye gather up the tares, ye root also the wheat with them. Let both grow together until the harvest: and in the time of harvest I will say to the reapers, Gather ye together first the tares, and bind them in bundles to burn them: but gather the wheat into my **barn. (Matthew 13:24-30) KJV**

Have you ever played a game and there were two pictures, but both of them looked identical? You than was asked to find the one that was a counterfeit? I have played some of these games, and you have to focus on both pictures to find the one that is not the real deal.

What this scripture is saying, is that there are counterfeits, that may appear to be a part of God's kingdom, but they are not. They are wolves in sheep's clothing, portraying themselves to be of God. Because sometimes our discernment is not as strong as we think that it is. Consequently, we sometimes see what we want. The closer that you walk with God the deeper your discernment will increase.

God gave some people a high level of discernment even though they may not know him, but they can see only in the natural realm.

Sometimes you will not be able to tell the wheat from the tares. Why? because they may both look exactly the same on surface.

We judge people by how they dress, talk, education, where they live, status and etc. Man looks on the outer appearance, but God looks at the heart. In addition, he knows those that are his, and when he returns, he will do the separating.

Moreover, you can't eat food from everyone's table. Therefore, you must ask God for discernment so that you will know truth from era.

Another important thing about seeking God is that you want to make your home a place where the spirit of God loves to dwell. Furthermore, your body is the actual place that God desires to make his abode, and if you are not attempting to sanctify yourself then you will just be a church goer. Therefore, this will affect your relationship with God as well.

For we wrestle not against flesh and blood, but against principalities, against powers, against the rulers of the darkness of this world, against spiritual wickedness in high places. **(Ephesians 6:12) KJV**

So now the adversary is using distractions such as technology. These devises have become an addiction for many people and some of them believe that this is the norm.

Why? Well, because almost everywhere you look someone has a cell phone or are on some type of technology. Therefore, thy believe that they are not obsessed because of this.

I once had a young lady tell me that her sister was so addicted to her cell phone, that she would sometimes wake up from her sleep to text someone. On the other hand, we know that some people have to use their cell phones for important reasons, such as their jobs, and emergency phone calls. but you don't want to make a god out of these things. Moreover, learn to call God because Jesus is on the main line, just tell him what you want.

For where two or three are gathered together in my name, there am I in the midst of them. **(Matthew 18:20) KJV**

This scripture is stating God can be reached in any place and at anytime and anywhere. Therefore, when you receive the Holy Ghost, you're the actual church. And where ever you go the church goes with you. **(Matthew 18:20)KJV**

There will be times when you may miss the mark, but don't worry about it. All you have to do is repent and keep it moving. However, satin will tell you that you made a mistake, and you might as well give up, don't fall for it. There are times when your flesh may get weak, but this (his is) natural because we are living in a sinful body. The Lord knows what we are going to do before we do it. It is no surprise to him when we fall short. This does not mean that he does not love us because we made a mistake. On the other hand, you don't want to willfully sin at least (but) up a good fight.

He's still molding and making us into his image. And if you have a mind to seek him then that is a blessing. Because he's the one that gave you the mind or the desire to serve him, even if you are not where you should be at this present time.

We sometimes will do worldly things, because we don't want people to think that we are better than they are. We also do worldly things because everyone else is doing it. It is not an abnormal thing to feel this way, because you have been programed by the worldly system almost all of your life.

This all starts at an early age without you being aware of it. Then there are times that some of us are aware of it, but remember the flesh likes to be satisfied and glorified. We are programmed, from television, school, music, friends, family, associations, clothing, and sometimes college.

All of these experiences help shape our thoughts, our patterns of how we do things, and also our belief. Unless God reveals himself to us we can easily be deceived. **(Matthew 24:24) KJV**

There are people believing that this scripture is saying that the elect can be deceived when this takes place. But if you read the verse above this one, you would notice that Jesus stated, for the elect's sake that he would shorten the days, because if he didn't shorten them, then no flesh would be saved.

Furthermore, you want to prepare your temple so that he can come and make his abode with you. because we want to abide with him forever. Nevertheless, the more you yield your members to God, the less things in this life will have an effect on you. As you get closer to God you learn to look at bad situations at a different perspective.

For the Lord himself shall descend from heaven with a shout, with the voice of the archangel, and with the trump of God: and the dead in Christ shall rise first: Then we which are alive and remain shall be caught up together with them in the clouds, to meet the Lord in the air: and so shall we ever be with the Lord. (1st Thessalonians 4:16 -18) KJV

Another thing that I want to say about serving God is that it is a personal salvation, therefore no matter how you may see other so-called Christians live their lives, should have nothing to do with your relationship with God. Therefore, you should be rooted and grounded in God, so that these things will not move you.

No one said that it would be easy Why? Because anything worthwhile usually will have a price tag attached to it. But as you continue to grow in the Lord you will began to notice that you are changing from a caterpillar to a butterfly. Consequently, this will eventually place because you are not allowing your flesh to dictate to you, nor push you around like it once did in the past. Of course, your flesh will fight to stay alive, but thanks be to God that gives us the victory through our Lord and Savior Jesus Christ.

Even Paul had problems with his flesh being at war and he was one of the greatest apostles that ever lived.

For the good that I would I do not: but the evil which I would not, that I do. Now if I do that I would not, it is no more I that do it, but sin that dwelleth in me.

O wretched man that I am! Who shall deliver me from the body of this death? **(Romans 7:14-2 5) KJV**

I thank God through Jesus Christ our Lord. So then with the mind I myself serve the law of God: but with the flesh the law of sin.

First, I need to explain to you what the word carnal means. When a person is carnal, they only are concerned with what they can see, smell, hear, taste or should I say their five senses. They also desire to satisfy their flesh which is called the old man. In other words, they are led by their senses and not by the Spirit of God. But the spiritual world does not operate in the same manner that the natural world does. In the spiritual world you have to walk by faith. and not by sight. In addition, a carnal minded person loves the things of the world and will follow the styles and customs of the world.

Love not the world, neither the things that are in the world. If any man love the world, the love of the Father is not in him. For all that is in the world, the lust of the flesh, and the lust of the eyes, and the pride of life, is not of the Father, but is of the world. **(1ˢᵗ John 2:15:29)KJV**

We should not dress, act, nor follow the ways of the world. This may be the reason why some people never receive the Holy Ghost, because

God will not dwell in an unclean temple and he has a holy nature. **(1ˢᵗ John 2:15-17)**

Have you ever experienced having an evil thought, but the image or the thought that came was very unusual for a person of your caliber? However, deep down in your heart you didn't want to do what your flesh was tempting you to do. You felt as if something was pulling you in a direction that you didn't desire to go. But it seemed as if you had no control over the situation. Everyone may not have experienced this in the same manner. It may have been that you've had an argument with someone, but You may not have wanted to say anything to make things worse. You then found yourself saying or doing the very thing that you didn't intend to do.

Some people go through this, but thy may not understand why it is happening to them. Some of these thoughts come from the adversary, and sometimes it could be your flesh that wants to be satisfied. On the other hand, it could be something that has crept into your heart and you didn't rebuke it. Moreover, there are times that you will have to talk to your flesh, to keep it under subjection as well.

The heart is deceitful above all things, and desperately wicked: who can know it? **(Jeremiah 17:9) KJV**

Keep thy heart with all diligence; for out of it are the issues of life. **(Proverbs 4:23) KJV**

The war does not stop just because you go to church and give God a few handclaps, so please don't get it twisted. The Holy Ghost will make a difference, but you must yield to it after receiving it. Receiving the Holy Ghost is the first step. You on the other hand must allow it to lead and guide you. consequently, an example of this would be like owning a bike but not know how to ride it.

I must mention that there are carnal minded saints that have received the Holy Ghost also. You must still work on your flesh after receiving the Holy Ghost. I guess you ask why? Well, because you're supposed to grow in the knowledge of our Lord and Savior Jesus.

We all need a comforter to fight for us, but we most fight the good fight of faith by fasting, staying in prayer, repenting, forgiving others, staying in God's presence, and studying the word of God.

The reason that we must forgive is that it can make us bitter when we don't. If God forgives us, we therefore, should forgive others.

And be ye kind one to another, tenderhearted, forgiving one another, even as God for Christ sake hath forgiven you. **(Ephesians 4:32) KJV**

Of course, if someone is your enemy this does not mean that you should turn a blind eye towards them.

Eat thou not the bread of him that hath an evil eye, neither desire thou his dainty meats: For as he thinketh in his heart, so is he: Eat and drink, saith he to thee; but his heart is not with thee. **(Proverbs 23:6-7)**

This just means that in your heart you should not hold bitterness nor try to get revenge.

In addition, let people say what they want to say about what God is doing in your life, because it could be that God has not revealed himself to them. Moreover, there could be some people that don't want you to grow and prosper, because they could be jealous of you.

There are some people that God has revealed certain things to pertaining to spiritual things, but this does not mean that he is finished with them. He could be using someone that may have a deeper revelation to help them grow.

Have you ever cooked a meal, but you took the food out oven too soon? You then placed the food back into the oven, so that it would continue cooking. Consequently, some people don't stay on the potter's wheel long enough, to allow God to finish working on them. Therefore, when trials and test come their way, thy are not able to endure, hardness as a good soldier.

Paul also mentioned that there was a war in his members, that was warring against the law of his mind and bringing him into captivity.

O wretched man that I am! who shall deliver me from the body of this death.

If you noticed, he called his temple the body of death.

Why? Because there is no good thing in our flesh. There are people that may not drink, smoke, fornicate and may be morally good people, but we were all born in sin and shaped in inequity, because when Adam and Eve disobeyed God in the garden of Eden they placed every human being born after them under condemnation. Remember, that Eve is the mother of all living, which means that we were born with an Adamic Nature.

We are taught in most churches that the building is the actual church, but this is not true. It is called a local assembly. This is where we go to feed our souls and to encourage one another. We also come to give the Lord praise and thank him for allowing us to see another day. Furthermore, we should keep the environment where we live as spiritual as possible. Because the time that we are living in, we need a shield of protection around us at all times.

The reason that I'm saying this is because how you live outside of the local assembly will have an effect on your spiritual growth as well.

The adversary does not mind you going to church, he just doesn't want you to bring the church home. In addition, you want to live a life that is pleasing in Gods sight. Because everyone will have to give an account for the deeds that are done in the body. Therefore, you must live right even if no one is watching you. But remember God sees all and he knows all, and what is done in the dark will come to the light.

What is the meaning of the word sanctification? It means that you are set apart for the master's use, consecrated and living a life of holiness.

Remember that some things in the natural world can be compared to in the spiritual. For example, when a person goes into the military, they have to be reprogramed to do what Uncle Sam tells them to do.

The first few weeks of training may be very difficult for some people, because they have been programmed by the ways of society. This is one reason some parents love when their children to go into the military, so that they can learn to be disciplined in this life. Of course, this may not work for everyone, because we all are created differently, but the military also can transform some people for their own good.

This also means that God has chosen you to be his servant, and you must please him instead of pleasing your flesh.

Sanctification is one of the most important steps to receiving the Holy Ghost after repentance. There are some people that may appear to be morally good. But there are other sins besides smoking drinking, fornicating, lying and stealing. There are inward sins that can't always be detected with the natural eye. Some people may have jealousy, envy, pride, fear, self-righteousness, bitterness, and being materialistic and may not be quite as noticeable. The Sins that can't be seen are called iniquity, because these sins become a part of the person' and don't need any type of temptation for it to surface. consequently, another way that a person can sanctify themselves, is to stop fornicating if they are not married.

*Flee fornication. Every sin that a man doeth is without body; but he that committeth fornication sinneth against his own body (**1st Corinthians 6:18)KJV***

Your body was not made for fornication but for the Lord. Therefore, you should flee fornication and wait for God to send you a mate. Furthermore, you should not marry someone that is a nonbeliever. But you should marry someone that is in the Lord as well.

There are some people that may have been delivered by the power of God from demon possession and the Lord has filled them with the Holy Ghost. Thus, if they continue to fornicate this could cause them to backslide. Why? Because one sin sometimes could lead to another. Therefore, the demons that thy were delivered from could return and bring with them seven more evil spirits worst then themselves. Therefore, the last state of that person would be worse than before.

He knows that we may fall short, but this particular sin could open up doors for other spirits, because we consist soul, spirit and dwell in a body. However, I stated that some people are more susceptible to demon spirits then others.

When the unclean spirit is gone out of a man, he walketh through dry places, seeking rest, and findeth none. Then he saith, I will return into my house from whence I came out; and when he is come, he findeth it empty, swept, and garnished. Then goeth he, and taketh with himself seven other spirits more wicked than himself, and they enter in and dwell there: and the last state of that man is worse than the first. Even so shall it be also unto this wicked generation. **(Matthew 12:43-45) KJV**

Another way that we can become sanctified is what we wear or apparel. I know that this will not be a very popular subject to expound on. But you have to remember I didn't write the bible, I'm only the messenger, and I'm conveying to you what has worked for me. However, it's just like in the military when a soldier doesn't want to obey orders, he then ends up being kicked out, because he don't want to obey orders.

It is the same thing in the spiritual realm. A lot of us don't like to be told what to do. Why is this? Well because we are born with the Adamic nature or in sin. Furthermore, we sometimes don't know how to surrender ourselves to God, because we may not have been taught, to know what God is requires of us. There are also times that we want to do things our way as well. We also need to guard our hearts and ask God to search us at all times.

Furthermore, you must be feed by someone that is in tune with God and is not just a motivational preacher. We sometimes like to sit under ministries that tickle our ears or tell us what we want to hear. You want to be in a ministry that can fed your spirit and teach you the word of God. But they also should be led by the Spirit of God in the services and allow God to take control of the services. You don't want to be somewhere where God is not allowed to have his way, or they don't care for God's presence.

In addition, you should want to learn more about the word of God and not just about Abraham, Isaac and Jacob every Sunday.

Also, there is a difference in reading the bible and studying the bible. **(2nd Timothy 2:15) KJV**

Of course, if you are a babe in Christ you want to learn the simple things at first, and then grow as time goes on.

Study to shew thyself approved unto God, a workman that needeth not to be ashamed, rightly dividing the word of truth. **(2ND Timothy 2:15) KJV**

Even the way that you dress can be a hinder in your relationship with God. Some people believe that it is not in what you wear, but that is not necessarily true.

We know that there are some people that may look holy on surface, but two wrongs never made a right. I know that you've heard that cliché before.

If you read the Old Testament and study it, you will notice that God had a law for everything that the children of Israel did, even down to how they were to dress. Well, I guess you say things has changed and that is somewhat true. On the other hand, this has not changed even though somethings's in the Old Testament has.

The first thing that people notice about you is your appearance, and remember you are supposed to be a representative of Christ. Therefore, you should not dress, act nor look like the world. How you present yourself could cause someone to lust after you and could cause both of you to fall. Remember we are still human and dwelling in a body of death. In addition, there is a war going on between the flesh and the Spirit.

Love not the world, neither the things that are in the world. If any man love the world, the love of the Father is not in him. For all that is in the world, the lust of the flesh, and the lust of the eyes, and the pride of life, is not of the Father, but is of the world. **(1st John 2:15-17) KJV**

You should not wear paints, makeup nor jewelry when seeking the Lord for the indwelling of his Spirit.

You should also realize that certain clothing, music, movies and some objects that reside in their homes may consist of evil spirits.

satin desires the women to take on the man's characteristics and he also desires the men to take on the women's. Why? Because satin is the god of this worldly system is jealous of God's creation.

In conclusion, he comes to conform man into the opposite of what God desires for them to be. He uses clothing, actions, morals, people's character, and etc.

The Lord was showing me that something was wrong in the spiritual realm, because most women hardly ever wear skirts or dresses. Consequently, when I was in the world, we wore paints once in a while. However, the styles were more feminine, and we had a more famine nature about us.

I realize that some people may not like dresses nor skirts, but it should not be almost the entire population.

God did not create a woman to have a man's nature, nor vice versa. We were not created to walk, sit, stand, nor to act a like man. In addition, he satin desires to sift all of us as wheat. He also wants you to call right wrong and wrong right. In fact, most of the things that I'm saying to you must be revealed to you by the Spirit of God, because the things that I'm speaking about is not of this world but comes from above. In addition, your flesh does not what you to change. Furthermore, if I don't tell you the truth then your blood will be on my hands.

There are times that we know that the things that we do are not pleasing in God's sight, but whatever, is popular is what most people will do. Furthermore, it doesn't matter if it is right or wrong.

Because straight is the gate, and narrow is the way, which leadeth unto life, and few there be that find it. **(Matthew 7:14) KJV**

The woman shall not wear that which pertaineth unto a man, neither shall a man put on a women's garment: for all that do so are abomination unto the Lord thy God. **(Deuteronomy 22:5)**

If you read the scripture in the book of Deuteronomy, you'll notice the word abomination is there and is pertaining to a woman wearing men's apparel. Remember we said the word abomination was something stinks or is rotten in Gods nostrils.

Did you know that you can be brain washed without knowing it, which is mind control? On the other hand, you have other's that are aware of what's going on in the spiritual realm. There are times that the flesh can overpower the person and they may not be able to help themselves. Moreover, you have other's that don't care to know about any of this.

The enemy is using music, clothing, technology, and even foods to destroy souls. In addition, a lot of the styles of the world was created by satin. It is just that he has to use a vessel to get his agenda done.

Remember we stated that satin is the god of this world, and there's spiritual wickedness in high places. Thereby, the adversary uses the people in high places to create ideas. An example of this would be music, clothing, colors, movies, cartoons, technology and ect. As a result, these ideas are passed down to the masses for his agenda.

This is why we should pray for one another because the spiritual war is about to escalate. However, there's a group that are called the Gothic satanic group, and they create styles that are very popular. They also love black clothing as well. This is the reason black clothing is in style as well. However, some of the styles crated by them appear to be innocent, therefore you would not believe that these styles were created by a satanic group of people. In addition, they also believe in dark clothing, black lips, black fingernail polish etc. you may not even be aware of what you are wearing or have in your home that is satanic as well. Why? Because thy produce bedspreads, shoes, paints, dresses, comforters, furniture, and even houses.

The Lord had revealed to me that something was wrong in the spiritual realm, because I didn't understand why so many people were wearing only black clothing most of the time.

I therefore decided to look deeper into it, and this is how I found out about this particular group.

You must remember satin loves darkness and he also knows that colors effect the mood of people without them realizing it. On the other hand, it is not the color that's the problem, but it is what is symbolizes in the spiritual realm. However now I see why the Lord says be in the world but not of it. He just didn't give us all of the details about how everything would take place, because he wants us to believe his word and trust him.

We are also in the Beast System, and most people are not even aware of it. Things in this world will become more satanic as time goes on. Also, people are being microchipped in various places around the world.

It will eventually be a requirement for every human being in the entire world to have a chip, implanted inside of their bodies. But in order for this to take place the cash will have to be done away with. In other words, this is called a cashless society. Moreover, my son had mentioned to me that he went into a store to purchase a smoothie, but when he went to pay for it the he was told that they did not except cash. Also, I had the same experience when I went to purchase some soup at another store. The cashier said that they did not take cash. However, I was astonished when he said this to me. He preceded to come from the back of the kitchen and told me that I could have the food.

First of all, your Flesh is at war with the ways of God, because it is our enemy. Second of all, there is a price to pay for salvation, and most people don't believe that it takes all of that. But I'm sorry to disappoint you, it takes that and some more to make this journey.

An example of this would be Jacob who had to wrestle with the angel all night long, before he got his blessing.

Everyone is always mentioning about Abraham being the father of nations, but no one hardly mentions the test that he had to go through to get the blessing. He was tested with his only son, that he loved. Of course, God had the angel to stop him before he killed him, and allowed a ram to be in the bush to use for a sacrifice instead of his son. Moreover, as you can see even Abraham had to pay for his blessing.

In other words, it is letting us know that there is a price to pay for anything worthwhile. If Jesus had to suffer whom am I.

if *any man will come after me, let him deny himself, and take up his* cross, and *follow me.*

The question is should Jesus bear the cross alone, and all the world go free, yes there's a cross for everyone and there's a cross for me?

Are you willing to fight for the blessing? Well it will be a fight, because we are in a warfare, but it will be worth it.

Now the kingdom of heaven suffereth violence, and the violent take it by force. ***(Matthew 11:12) KJV***

For we wrestle not against flesh and blood, but against principalities, against powers, against the rulers of the darkness of this world, against spiritual wickedness in high places. ***(Ephesians 6:12) KJV***

I can remember when I was seeking the Lord for the Holy Ghost, I therefore had to go on a three day and night fast, because the bible says that

Howbeit this kind goeth not out but by prayer and fasting. ***(Matthew 17:21) KJV***

You must seek the Lord not just while you are in the local assembly, but it should be a way of life. But until you become hungry and thirsty for more of God you will most likely remain the same.

This is why God sometimes allows our world to be turned upside down. One reason that he allows this is, because we can become too comfortable in this life, especially when things are going smoothly for us.

Another reason that God allows this is, because he desires for us to always need him. Furthermore, I can remember when I was coming out of a very difficult test, and the Lord spoke into my spirit, and said to me when you come out of this situation you're have more things to go through, because I want you to always need me.

My desire to find God acceded my necessity to eat food. This will sometimes occur when the Lord is dealing with you constantly or above normal, However, when this is happening to you, nothing on this earth will satisfy you.

We now have another problem in these last and evil days, because the enemy is using distractions as never before

However, People in these last days love to be entertained. Therefore, they will even find a church that will satisfy their fleshly desires. I believe that this sometimes happens because the flesh is waring against the Spirit, and sometimes people are not aware of what is going on. Consequently, on the service these particular things appear to be very harmless, but this is a spiritual warfare and the enemy desires to sip every one of us as wheat. Moreover, God cannot deal with you as much as he would like to, because you are so caught up in technology or things of this world.

Even if a person doesn't believe in God being obsessed with anything could be a hinder to them. Especially if they have an artistic gift that God has given them. Remember also that gifts and callings are without repentance. **(Romans 11:29) KJV**

People that have these particular gifts need to sometimes get away to themselves and be in a quite atmosphere or near nature. Therefore, when you slow down and take time out for yourself, things can sometimes be revealed to you, that you never thought of.

I'm not saying that technology is all bad, but society have made a god of these things.

Why is this happening? One reason that this is taking place is, because man was created to serve the one and only true living God. But when we don't serve him, then we will find something else to take the place of what we were created for.

It could be drinking, sex, drugs, materialistic things, money, technology, sports and ect.

Don't think that the enemy will not tell you that I don't know what I, m talking about, because remember this is a warfare and he don't fight fair. Moreover, the more you learn and get to know about God the more you will love him, and satin knows that.

We must also keep the door of our lips, because this is the hardest part of the body for us to tame. Even after you to know God, this will sometimes be the hardest part of the body to keep under control, especially if you are an outspoken person.

For in many things we offend all. If any man offend not in word, the same is a perfect man, and able also to bridle the whole body. (JAMES 3:2- 12) KJV

Have you ever been in an argument with someone and it seemed that the more you said the angrier that you became? It sometimes can turn into a fight as well. In addition, when you keep talking you are not listing to what the other person is saying, especially if you are waiting to get in the last word in the conversation. And if you take time to listen long enough, you will sometimes find out what's on the other person's heart.

There are times when even the smallest things can turn into a serious conflict, if you continue adding fuel to the fire.

Sometimes the person may not be angry at you, they may be angry about a situation in their lives. On the other hand, if they are hungry, tired, and had a bad day even the smallest argument could escalate into something serious if you keep talking. If you want to find out what the problem could be, you should wait until they are in a better frame of mind, to approach them. Consequently, you must remember that satin is the author of confusion.

But there will be times that you may need to get something off of your chest. Because if you have an aught against someone than you should go to them. But you must therefore pray and let your words be seasoned with grace. Don't use words like you did this, or you should have done that. You should talk about the situation but not the person. Nor do any blaming. If they don't want peace in the conversation, then just keep quit and let God take care of it.

Moreover, if thy brother shall trespass against thee, go and tell him his fault between thee and him alone: if he shall hear thee, thou hast gained thy brother. But if he will not hear thee, then take with thee one or two more, that in the mouth of two or three witnesses every word may be established. (**Matthew 15) KJV**

There are some people that may have it out for you, and you most of the time you will know who they are. In reality they are being used by the power of darkness and are just vessels to pull you down. Sometimes when you're trying to get closer to God things may seem to get worse instead of better. This is because when satin see that you are trying to get closer to God, he wants to stop you before you get to know him.

God can bless you with a nice house, car, and a good job. These things are nice to have while you are here on earth, but they're only temporal and not eternal. But what God places inside of your soul is eternal and satin knows this. If you notice, we are living in a very materialistic world, and most people are caught up in materialistic things.

Beloved, I wish above all things that thou mayest prosper and be in health, even as thy soul prospereth. (3rd John 1-2) KJV

You see were God said that he wanted us to prosper and *be in good health, even as thy soul propereth.* What does this mean? It means that God desires for us to prosper but don't place prosperity above your soul. You see your soul is more precious than silver and gold. However, we are living in a time where people seem to be more concerned about materialistic things then their health as well. Why? Because it is the popular thing to do. In addition, some people are on their way to bad health and don't see never it is coming. They don't see it coming because they feel like everything Is ok, but there are some sicknesses that take place gradually. If satin can get you to not take care of your temple, he knows that he can destroy you faster. In addition, most of the money that people have accumulated will go back into the system for doctor visits, medications, and medical bills. Consequently, you only have one life, therefore you must take care of your temple. However, we know that most of us don't eat the way that we should at all times, but when you miss the mark you should at least take breaks from eating junk foods. Moreover, you should educate yourself about how to take more care of yourself. Why? Because your natural man will affect your spiritual man. In fact, when you don't feel good, it can affect your mood and how well you think.

Have you ever visited a church but found that the people were not what you anticipated them to be? What You must realize, serving God is an individual thing for all of us. And no one can judge me by what other's do.

Everyone that comes to church is not in the actual church. Even though, some of them may have titles and positions, this does not mean that they are all walking as they should. Because you will know a tree by the fruit, and not by there title.

Then there are some people that God is not with and is still molding them. Please be patient with them. Why? Because God not be through with them Yet.

Let's for example take someone that is baking a cake. God may still have that person in the oven, and he may have to turn the heat up to get their attention.

There are some people that come to church looking for a reason not to serve the Lord, and there are some that have been wounded. This is why you need to be rooted and grounded in God, because we will have no excuse on judgment day.

*But in a great house there are not only vessels of gold and of silver, but also of wood and of earth; and some of honor, and some of dishonor. If a man therefore purge himself from these, he shall be a vessel unto honor, sanctified, and meet for the master's use, and prepared unto every good work. (2nd **Timothy 2:20-22**)*

Therefore, let the wheat and tares grow together and when God comes, he will do the separating.

The reason why the lord said this is, because if you look at wheat and tares, they both look similar. Therefore, you may think that the wheat is a tare, but it could be the opposite of what you see. The tares may look good on the outside but is poison on the inside.

This is how we sometimes prejudge people by how they dress, talk, where they live and what they may drive. No one can discern everyone and know what's in their hearts, because we are not God. It is just that some of us judge people by outward appearances only. We should not judge anyone, unless it is righteous judgement.

The enemy can also transform himself into an angel of light. How? Because he was once a Cherub Angel in heaven and knows what it is like to be in God's presence. He does not always expose himself, because he sometimes likes to be hidden. Moreover, he may have charisma, charm, education, may be attractive, may be religious, and may have worldly wisdom. In addition, because of this it is sometimes hard to discern this particular spirit, unless the Lord reveals it to you. On the other hand, sometimes God does reveal certain things to us, but we sometimes see what we want to as well.

The adversary also knows the word of God, but he can't live it. An example of this, would be when the devil tried to tempt our Lord and Savior, after he had fasted for forty days and forty nights.

Then the devil taketh him up into the holy city, and setteth him on a pinnacle of the temple, And saith unto him, if thou be the Son of God, cast thyself down: for it is written, He shall give his angels charge concerning thee: and in their hands they shall bear thee up, lest at any time thou dash thy foot against a stone. **(Matthew 4:5)KJV**

As you can see the devil uses the words for it is written, because he knows the word. Furthermore, he is quoting Psalm 91 to Jesus. He will also tell you part truth and part lies.

He that dwelleth in the secret place of the most High shall abide under the shadow of the Almighty. **(Psalm 91:11)**

And no marvel; for satin himself is transformed into an angle of light. (2nd **Corinthians 11:14) KJV**

The enemy also know that people have itchy ears in these last and evil days. This means that they don't want to change. Therefore, he will tell you want you want to hear which about only prosperity and blessings.

There are people that may look down on other's because they may not use the correct words when they talk or may not have as much education as they may have. But you may never know what it took for that person to be where they are now. There is a saying that people use to say walk a mile in my shoes.

Remember tares are counterfeits that may look similar to the wheat, and you therefore, cannot always identify the one from the other. You will not know, unless the lord reveals or uncovers the real person behind the mask. **(Matthew 13:24-24)KJV**

However, there is no perfect human being on this earth, and we all fall short at times or miss the mark. Therefore, we must love people no how they treat us.

This does not mean that you should not protect yourself, if you know that they are your enemy. If that is the case, then you should try to stay away from that person as much as possible. But your real enemy is satin that is using them to fight against you, and they are just vessels being used to bring you down.

Because greater is he that is in you, then he that is in the world. (1st John 4:4) **KJV**

There is nothing new under the sun, because this happened when David wanted Uriah to be killed because he had impregnated his wife Bathsheba.

The Lord sent Nathan, which was a prophet to David because of the evil that he had done against Uriah.

And the Lord sent Nathan unto David. And he came unto him, and said unto him, There were two men in one city; the one rich, and the other poor. The rich man had exceeding many flocks and herds: But the poor man had nothing, save one little ewe lamb, which he had bought and nourished up: and it grew up together with him, and with his children; it did eat of his own meat, and drank of his own cup, and lay in his bosom, and was unto him as a daughter. And there came a traveller unto the rich man, and he spared to take of his own flock and of his own herd, to dress for the wayfaring man that was come unto him; but took the poor man's lamb, and dressed it for the man that was come to him. And David's anger was greatly kindled against the man; and he said to Nathan, As the Lord liveth, the man that hath done this thing shall surely die: And he shall restore the lamb fourfold, because he did this thing, and because he had no pity. And Nathan said unto David, Thou art the man. (2nd Samuel 12:1-7)kjv

In this story David's men were at war, but he didn't participate in the war with them. He decided to take a walk on the roof top of his palace. While there, he notices a beautiful woman that was bathing. Her name was Bathsheba the mother of Solomon. But he could not get her off of his mind, therefore he makes inquiries about her, and finds out that she is the wife of Uriah the Hittite. Of course, Uriah was at war fighting the Ammonites. David than sends for her, and then commits adultery with her. He later finds out that she is with child. But now he is in more trouble because he has to cover his tracks. David now sends for Uriah her husband and attempts to get him to sleep with his wife Bathsheba, but Uriah felt it a dishonor to go into his wife while his men were fighting the Ammonites. He would've also been violating the Israelites rule that apply for warriors, if he had gone into his wife.

David tricks Uriah into getting drunk, while having dinner with him. Then Uriah falls to sleep and lies down, but the next morning David sends a note to Joab the captain of the army, by the hands of Uriah. The note stated that Joab was to place Uriah on the front line for war. The motive for this was increase his chances of being killed. Finally, David's plane was accomplished, and Uriah was eventually killed. Then David took Bathsheba, and she became his wife.

Also, unbelief is a sin and can hinder your growth spiritually. Consequently, anything that you do in unbelief is classified as a sin, even though it may not be. An example of this would be someone that may believe Saturday's should be a day of worship. Therefore, it is classified as a sin only because they believe that it is.

Let no man therefore judge you in meat, or in drank, or in respect of an holyday, or of the new moon, or of the sabbath days: Which are a shadow of things to come; but the body is of Christ. (Colossians2:16) KJV

Beware lest any man spoil you through philosophy and vain deceit, after the tradition of men, after the rudiments of the world, and not after Christ.

Faith is a very powerful way to get God to move in your life. This may be one of the reasons that we don't receive certain things from the Lord, because of unbelief. We may have faith in one area, but not in another.

But without faith it is impossible to please him: for he that cometh to God must believe that he is, and that he is a rewarder of them that diligently seek him **(Hebrews 11)**

Ask, and it shall be given you; seek, and ye shall find; knock, and it shall be opened unto you: For every one that asketh receiveth; and he that seeketh findeth; and to him that knocketh it shall be opened. (**Matthew 7:7) KJV**

Ye ask, and receive not, because ye ask amiss, that ye may consume it upon your lust.

Moreover, if you don't have enough faith seek the Lord, and he will give it to you.

Chapter 6

The Power of Fasting and Prayer

Why do we need to fast and pray? For one thing fasting will help crucify some of your fleshly desires. Some people may not be able to fast the same way as others because of illnesses or diseases. But you could do a fast that consist of omitting meats and sweets. However, it's up to you to decide what is good for you and to allow the Lord to lead you into what to do.

You should consult your doctor before attempting to do anything as far as fasting, when you are on any type of medications.

But for those of us that are in good health we can fast sometimes. The word of God says:

Is not this the fast that I have chosen: to loose the bands wickedness, to undo the heavy burdens, and to let the oppressed go free, and that ye break every yoke?

There will always be something for you to fast for, as long as we are in this flesh, because we are in a warfare. Fasting may also help keep your flesh under subjection, but you must do it the correct way. On the other hand, your flesh is not your friend, even though most of us are more concerned about natural man then we then we are about the inner man.

You can also do a liquid fast, whereby you may desire to omit foods, but drink only water and fluids. There is another type of fast that is called a dry fast. This particular fast means that you don't eat nor drink anything whatsoever.

There are times in your life that you may need to go on an extreme fast, especially if you need a lot of yokes to be broken in your life. Sometimes the more extreme fast could led to a more extreme blessing. But you must use wisdom and know when it is time to eat.

I believe that if I hadn't gone on a three fast days and night fast before I received the Holy Ghost, I may have never gotten the victory. I needed so many yokes broken in my life, and they are still being broken.

Sometimes there may be generational curses that may also need to be broken in your life. This does not mean that you are a bad person, it's just the way life is sometimes.

But even after fasting and prayer and being faithful I still had to be consistent in my endeavors of seeking the Lord. 1234 But e1ven after th1e fast I sti111ooooll had to fi111

Is it such a fast that I have chosen? a day for a man to afflict his soul? Is it to bow down his head as a bulrush, and to spread sackcloth and ashes under him? wilt thou call this a fast, and an acceptable day to the Lord? Is not this the fast that I have chosen? to loose the bands of wickedness, to unto the heavy burdens, and to let the oppressed go free, and that ye break every yoke? Is it not to deal thy bread to the hungry, and that thou bring the poor that are cast out to thy house? when thou seest the naked, that thou cover him; and that thou hide not thyself from thine own flesh? Then shall thy light break forth as the morning, and thine health shall spring forth speedily; and thy righteousness shall go before thee; the glory of the Lord shall be thy reward.

Then shalt thou call, and the Lord shall answer; thou shalt cry, and he shall say, Here I am. If thou take away from the midst of thee the yoke, the putting forth of the finger, and speaking vanity; And if thou draw out thy soul to the hungry, and satisfy the afflicted soul; then shall they light rise in obscurity, and thy darkness be as the noon day: And the Lord shall guide thee continually, and satisfy thy soul in drought, and make fat thy bones: and thou shalt be like a watered garden, and like a spring of water, whose waters fail not.

What does it mean to break every yoke? A yoke in the natural is a wooden is a wooden crosspiece that is fastened over the neck of two animals, to do a certain job. The animal must be guided by someone, in order for this to be accomplished.

What was sackcloth and ashes? Sackcloth was a piece of clothing that people wore when they were in mourning. This particular item was made out of course material, and people would sometimes rip the material to relieve stress.

The yoke of sin is sometimes very heavy. Why? Because you are caring your own burdens, and you are being guided by your natural mind instead of being guided by the Spirit of God.

This is why some people commit suicide, drink, and do drugs, because there is an emptiness inside, that these things cannot satisfy. Sometimes they are not aware of why they are going through these changes.

I can remember when I was in sin, that I would always walk with my head down, because I always felt as if I was caring the weight of the world on my shoulders. After I found the Lord, I still was under extreme pressure, but I had unspeakable joy in the mist of the storm. that took me through. Moreover, we call the Holy Ghost a comforter, but it is much more than that. However, when I was in the world, I indulged in drinking, dancing and various other things. But I always had an emptiness inside of me that I couldn't explain.

It is not the fact that I hadn't gone to church, because I would go ever Sunday with my foster mother. But This particular church was not teaching me what I needed to know about God. It was more like a form of godliness and being at a social gathering. However, when you're in sin you sometimes don't recognize why you do the things that you do, especially if the people around you are doing worldly things.

Take my yoke upon you, and learn of me; for I am meek and lowly in heart: and ye shall find rest for your souls. (Matthew 11:29-30) KJV

What he is really saying is that you will still go through things, and may have some bumps but, the ride will be much smoother if you allow the Lord to take the wheel.

In life there will be temptations, test, and trials Why? *Man that is born of a woman is of a few days, and full of trouble.* (**Job 14:1:5**) **KJV**

In addition, God allows things so that we will always need him, and he don't want us to become too comfortable in this life. Why? Because it is not really our home we are just passing through. On the other hand, temptation is common to man and there is nothing new under the sun.

There are many things that God will do for you if you seek him with your whole heart. Also, if you fast the correct way God will loose the band of wickedness, allow the oppress to go free, and he will break every yoke. This is called a day for a man to afflict his soul.

I guess you say why we should fast? The reason that we fast is because we have an outer man and an inner man that are at war with each other. Therefore, we want to kill out the old man and strengthen the inner one. Because the inner man is the one that wants God, but your outer man does not desire him.

When we fast, we should also do something special for someone that is in need a well.

And the Lord shall guide thee continually, and satisfy they soul In drought, and make fat thy bones: and thou shalt be like a watered garden, and like a spring of water, whose waters fail not. **(Isaiah 58:11)**

Another thing that you shouldn't do during your fast is to let others know that you are not eating. I guess you wonder why I would mention this? Well, one of the reasons, that I mentioned this is because the flesh sometimes can cause you to feel self-righteous about what you are doing. However, this is just the works of the flesh and how it operates. When you mention to someone that you are fasting you've already received your reward, because you have just glorified your flesh.

Also, during your fast if you have an aught against someone you should forgive them, and if you have to confront them you should not confront them while you're on your fast.

For if ye forgive men their trespasses, your heavenly Father will also forgive you. **(Matthew 6:14) KJV**

Moreover when ye fast, be not, as the hypocrites, of a sad countenance: for they disfigure their faces, that they may appear unto men to fast. Verily I say unto you, They have their reward. But thou, when thou fastest, anoint thine head, and wash they face; That thou appear not unto men to fast, but unto thy Father which is in secret: and thy Father, which seeth in secret, shall reward thee openly. **(Matthew 6:15-18) KJV**

You must remember after coming off of a long fast that you should not consume heavy foods, but you should ease your way back into eating them. In other words, you should know how to come off of a fast so that you will not get sick. Try to not to eat foods that are too heavy at first. But try eating light foods such as soups, try juicing fruits or vegetables, warm drinks, or vegetables. However, I've never fasted no more than three days and a half. but you must be led by the Spirit what you should do.

There may be times that the Lord will put you on a fast. I guess you say how will know? Well, the more you get to know him the more you're understand some of his ways. I can since when he places me on a fast even then your flesh may still desire to eat. One way that I can tell that he is leading on a fast is because I will have lots of energy and will not feel thirsty. Sometimes God will do this to prepare you for a test to come as well. You should also know when it time to end your fast, just use common sense.

While you are fasting, you should do less talking as much as possible unless you have to. But mainly try to fast from technology such as Facebook, television, texting. However, you should try to spend some quality time with the Father, whenever possible. In addition, you should not just read the bible but, you also want to study and meditate on it as well.

I must also mention to you that if you are married, that you should consult your partner, that you are going on a fast, so that they will understand why you are not coming together with them. What I'm saying is biblical But, don't overdo this because satin may use this to tempt your mate to go outside of the marriage.

After coming to God there would be times when the lord would deal with me in my sleep. He would place a inspirational song in my spirit to prepare me for a tremendous test. Therefore, when the song would be played on the radio the Spirit of God would fall heavily on me. The first reason, that the Lord sometimes operates like this is to strengthen the inner man. The second reason is because the joy of the Lord is our strength. In addition, this is how he manifests his power, because without him we can do nothing.

This is why satin don't mind going through the motion when you're praising God. He doesn't care about you giving God two or three handclaps. In fact, he will use other people to make you think something is wrong with you, because you are glorifying God. Thereby, they may not be as hungry for God in the same manner that you are. On the other hand, it could be that this part of God has not been revealed to them as well.

Some people may believe that serving God should be a casual thing, but it takes that and some more to win the warfare that we are in. Therefore, we must use all of the all the ammunition that the Lord has given us.

Also, you don't want to be a saint that only focuses on jumping and shouting which is wonderful if God falls on you in that manner, because the bible says quince not the Spirit. But you want to learn his word and get to know him for yourself. Likewise, you should also love Gods' presence just like you love his word as well.

*God is a Spirit: and they that worship him must worship him in Spirit and in truth. (**John 4:24) KJV***

There was a prophet, that was in the Old Testament, whose name was Isiah. He was sent to warn the Israelites about judgement that was coming upon them Why? Because they were a very rebellious people just like a lot of us, nevertheless they had been slaves in Egypt for four hundred and thirty years and had taken on some of their presumptuous ways. As result of this some of them were idol worshipers.

Sometimes God shows his power through people that are the least likely to succeed in this life. For instance, they may be weak, uneducated, unloved, and despised and ect.

But God hath chosen the foolish things of the world to confound the wise; and God hath chosen the weak things of the world to confound the things which are mighty; And base things of the world, and things which are despised, hath God chosen, yea, and things which are not, to bring to nought things that are: That no flesh should glory in his presence. **(1st Corinthians 1:27)** KJV

We have to remember that everyone goes through something in life, but some people may never have had a brake, nor a support system while they were going through.

This is sometimes why some people that have gone through extreme pressures in life, may also have a more intense praise, then those that have had light afflictions. people may think that there're acting when there're praising. They don't realize that if they weren't praising him, they might have lost their minds. Why? Because you don't know their story and don't know what they've gone through and could be going through as well. In addition, it could be that they remember where God had brought them from, and they appreciate what he has done in their lives. Furthermore, you may be judging them without knowing their story, even though you may not care to know. In addition, there have been times in my life that all I had was a praise.

On the other hand, in some cases going through in this life may not always be a curse, it can also be a blessing. Why? Because, you get to know what it feels like to suffer and can identify with someone else that is going through the similar situations. In fact, we sometimes need trials and tribulations to keep us humble, and so that we will not think that we are better than others.

Some of the yokes that may need to be broken while you're on fasting could be gluttonous, talking too much, alcoholism, sickness, depression, poverty, generational curses, sexual sins, jealousy, bitterness, unforgiveness, and the list goes on and on.

In fact, you can always talk to your heavenly Father about your problems and whatever, you're going through. In addition, you can also acknowledge that you are feeling discouraged or even being tempted. Why? Because this is a part of life, and temptation is common to man. Moreover, you're living in a natural world and attempting to prepare for the next one. In conclusion, this can be very difficult to try to balance both.

And he said unto me, My grace is sufficient for thee: for my strength is made perfect in weakness. Most gladly therefore will I rather glory in my infirmities, that the power of Christ may rest upon me. Therefore I take pleasure in infirmities, in reproaches, in necessities, in persecutions, in distresses for Christ's sake: for when I am weak, then am I strong. (**11corinthians12:9-10**)

The Lord is aware that we need his help, and that we cannot make this journey on our own. He is pleased when we acknowledge our faults and come to him with an open heart. Sometimes we want to tell ourselves that we can handle it alone, but that is not always true. We have to realize that God is all powerful and there is nothing too hard for him.

Actually, God knows everything before it takes place. He knew you in your mother's womb and knew everything that you would face in this world. Life is only a test, but it is how you view it. Furthermore, it is Just like when you were in school and sometimes the teacher would give you a pop quiz. Then there were other times that they told you that a test was going to take place. Moreover, this is similar to how life is in the natural, because you never know how you will be tested, nor do you know when it will take place. In fact, this one of the reasons that we should keep our minds on the Lord.

Thou wilt keep him in perfect peace, whose mind is stayed on thee: because he trusteth in thee. **(Isahia 26:3) KJV**

In addition, he will never put more on you than you can bear.

There are other reasons why we sometimes go through so much in this life. In fact, it could be because of the choices, that we've made. But we don't always want to admit it to ourselves, and as a result, we have to sometimes reap what we have sawn.

If you read the story of David after he committed adultery with Bathsheba, he still had to pay for his sins, even though God forgiven him. But, God told him that he was going to raise up trouble in his house hole because of disobedience.

This is why his son Absalom tried to kill him and slept with his concubines on the roof top in front of all of Israel. In addition, the child that Bathsheba was pregnant with God didn't permeant the child to live, even though David fasted and prayed about the situation. (**2ⁿᵈ Samuel 12:11) KJV**

It is only by God's grace and mercy that we will make it through this warfare. Also, if life is taking a toll on you then you can always go to your heavenly Father and cry out to him, even though he already knows about your situation. However, he loves it when you come to him with your problems, he loves you, and he wants you to depend on him at all times. go to him this. On the other hand, satin will tell you lies to get you to give up on God because you made a mistake. He doesn't want you to have a deep relationship with the Father.

There are times that you may believe that you can handle life on your own and you may tell yourself that nothing is bothering you but the Lord wants you to acknowledge him in all if your ways.

It would be nice if you could find another person that is on the same page that you are to talk to, at various times about God. But you should seek God about whom that person should be. Why? One reason that I've mentioned this is because, even though the Lord may be dealing with them as well, they may not desire to know him on the same level as you. Another reason is they may discourage you because you may not know that much about God and his word. This therefore could confuse you and could cause you to stop seeking the Lord the way that you should

Remember that I said that the carnal mind cannot understand spiritual things. On the other hand, you don't want to fellowship with someone that is always complaining or gossiping about others. Of course, they may sometimes mention something that they may be going through, but it should not be on an ongoing basis. In addition, you want to fellowship with someone that loves to pray and have the same mind that as you in seeking the Lord. In addition, if you fellowship with the wrong person it could have an effect on what the Lord is trying to do in your life. Even, a person that is spiritually minded can be pulled back if they fellowship on a continuous basis with a carnal minded person. However, this is not saying that you should not talk to that person or act like you're better than they are. But you must pray and ask God for wisdom on how to handle the situation, and if they are having an effect on your spiritual life, then you must withdraw yourself from them if it is possible.

On the other hand, if you can't find the right person, you're better off walking alone. Also ask God to send you to a church where you can grow in him. However, when you are new to the ways of God, or a babe in Christ don't allow them to use you to work in the church while God is dealing with you. Why? Because you will be focused more on working in the church building instead of focusing on God's word and getting to learn about his ways.

Blessed is the man that walketh not in the counsel of the ungodly, nor standeth in way of sinners, nor sitteth in the seat of the scornful. But his delight is in the law of the Lord; and in his law doth he meditate day and night. **(Psalms 1) KJV**

Another thing that you should know that you will not find a perfect church because no one is perfect, but we all must give account to God for ourselves.

You must seek God if no one else does, because everyone may not have the same hunger for God. Don't think that just because people are in the church building that they are all of God.

Now let's talk about prayer which is another weapon to fight satin. This may be one of hardest thing for most people to concur. Why? because your flesh does not desire for you to pray, and there are many distractions to detour you from praying.

Then there are times that the adversary may also cause you to feel sleepy while you're reading your bible. If you find yourself not able to sleep at night just get your bible and read it.

The Lord will sometimes wake you up out of sleep so that you can pray, because there could be a hard test coming your way and he may want you to prepare you for it. Remember we are in a warfare.

You also don't have to worry about trying to use extravagate words to empress God when you are praying because he's not concerned about that.

On the other hand, the first thing that you should do when praying is to give God thanks, even if you are going through something. I guess you're saying why should I do this, when I'm feeling so low in my spirit? Well, one reason that you should do this is because you need his strength to get you through your season of testing.

There will be different seasons in your life, just like it is in the natural. Therefore, you will have trials and tribulations because it is a part of life. Furthermore, weather you serve God or not has nothing to do with life having its up's and down's. However, having God in your life will make it lot easier to deal with it. On the other hand, if you run ahead of God you could miss your season of blessings. **(Ecclesiastes 3) KJV**

*Pray without ceasing. In everything give thanks: for this is the will of God in Christ Jesus concerning you. Quench not the Spirit. (***1st Thessalonians 5:17) KJV**

These are truly the end times and the gentile dispensation may be coming to a close. In fact, we should fast and pray even more in these parlous times.

What is the meaning of the word dispensation? Well a dispensation is the time period that God allows man to repent, and to be saved from the wrath which is to come.

There are seasons in your life that you may not have the time to seek the Lord. But you still should try to squeeze in some time for the Lord instead of spending so much time on social media. On the other hand, there are times when satin will try to keep you so busy doing things that are not important. Why? Because he knows that we are only here on earth for only a season, and once we lose time, we cannot get it back. Moreover, he will also use people to overload you, especially if you hate to say no to them. You must know your boundaries and listen to your body. On the other hand, there's nothing wrong with a person staying busy to a certain degree because they may need this to keep themselves out of trouble or to accomplish something important. But there are seasons that we should spend some quality time with the Lord to seek his face and to know his will. Besides I know that everyone's situation is not the same, but you know what your circumstances are. This is just for people that fit this profile.

But if our gospel be hid, it is hid to them that are lost: in whom the god of this world hath blinded the minds of them which believe not, lest the light of the glorious gospel of Christ, who is the image of God, should shine unto them. (2ⁿᵈ **Corinthians 4:3-4)**

This just means that satin is the god of this worldly system. This is why God told us to be in the world but not of it. What he is saying have no fellowship with the power of darkness such as the music, styles, dancing, drinking, fornication, lying, cheating, and what we watch with our eyes, which are the works of the flesh.

I've been watching some of the children's cartoons and have been noticing satin slipping satanic images into them. These images are so subtle that you barely will be aware of what he's doing. In addition, he is using subliminal messages to capture the children's minds. But if you must ask God to open up your spiritual eyes, so that you're recognize what he is attempting to do. Although we know that he's sometimes come as a wolf in sheep clothing.

What is the meaning of subliminal messages? The meaning of this word is below the threshold. This means that it is unnoticed. This takes place through commercials, cartoons, movies, and ect. Therefore, people are being controlled by subliminal messages on a regular basis.

Most styles and various music that people listen to are created by people that are in high places, and the prince and powers of darkness govern them. Then the ideas are passed down to the public. Most people are not aware of what is getting inside of their spirits, and there are others that don't care to know.

Some people are aware about what is going on, but they are concerned about what others may think of them, and they don't want to be a reject in society.

But those that are sold out to God must suffer persecution, because this is another way to be identified with Christ. **(1st John 2-15-17) KJV**

On the other hand, fasting and prayer are very powerful tools to fight the enemy. But your flesh will still try to eat even when you are not hungry. Therefore, you will have to put up a fight against the craving for foods. Also, there will be times that you will not feel like praying. But if you just do it by faith sometimes God will really come by and bless you. Also, the key to praying is to come out of self and let the Lord take control of you. Consequently, most people like to be in control of everything, but when you are in God's presence you want him to take charge because he will not harm you. However, he will not force himself on you if you don't desire his presence. But you want him to take control of your life. In addition, you want to break through the demonic forces that are fighting you. Likewise, your flesh wants to hold you in bondage.

I guess you say how should I pray? Well you can start off with the Lord's prayer. For instance, I sometime listen to spiritual music while in prayer and also while I'm exercising. This actually helps me to get my mind off of things in this present world. Not to mention, you may have had a day that was not going so well. However, this will sometimes happen, because this it is a part of life. Moreover, there are days that you may feel discouraged. Whenever, this takes place you should let the lord know how you are feeling, because he already knows. In fact, you may even feel like literally crying in tears unto the Lord, because he is the best friend that you will ever have. You therefore, should just let the tears flow.

You can also start your prayers off with praises as well. Likewise, you should ask God for forgiveness, because we all fall short in this life, because life can be very trying at times. Besides you should let him know what your needs are.

Also, if you ask the Lord to make and mold you, then you should expect to be tested and tried. Why? Because the bible says tribulation worketh patience. Even in the spiritual realm you will not get something for nothing. **(Romans 5:3) KJV**

Remember we said that the natural world is sometimes similar to the spiritual. It is similar to exercising your body at the gym. You do this so that you can make your body fit, and also be in good health. You must also exercise to get the result that you desire. Therefore, if you desire more patience, and want to be molded by God, then you must tried by the fire.

Also, there is a difference between praying in the Spirit, and praying in the flesh. This is not saying that God does not hear you when you pray, it is just that when you have the Holy Spirit inside It will sometimes help you pray Why? Because we don't always know what to pray for, and the Spirit also knows what is ahead. There will be times when you should listen to what God wants to speak into your spirit, and allow him to minister unto you as well.

Likewise the Spirit also helpeth our infirmities: for we know not what we should pray for as we ought: but the Spirit itself maketh intercessions for us with groanings which cannot be uttered. ***(Romans 8:26) KJV***

Let me explain to you what an infirmity is. It could be a physical or spiritual weakness. A physical weakness could a sickness a mental weakness, depression and various other things.

The word intercession means someone that stands proxy for another person or intervenes for them.

None of us are worthy of God's grace and mercy, and if God was to mark inequity who would stand, for all have sinned and fallen short of God's glory. On the other hand, this does not mean that we should use these scriptures for an excuse to sin and to trample over Gods mercy.

What does it mean by groanings that cannot be uttered? This is talking about when someone is praying in the Spirit and the Holy Ghost takes over the prayer. The Spirit of God will intercede for them with groanings. Because we don't know what is coming in the future. Besides, God knows what's ahead of us, and it may not always be shown to us by the Spirit.

We should also watch as well as pray because sometimes our discernment is not very sharp. Most people have some discernment but there are different levels of it.

Discernment is the ability to know truth from error and not judge by appearance. When you grow in God, as you should this quality should increase because everyone has it. Some people may not have as much as others.

Even most animals can discern people or things that are about to happen. Sometimes on the news you will see where some of animals will sense something in nature that is about to take place, and they will therefore go to high ground for safety and the humans will not pick on what is about to take place.

Look how great God is to even give animals a since of discernment for things to come.

What a mighty God we serve, even the animals are more in tune with him more than some of us.

Chapter 7

The Different Operations of the Holy Spirit

There are a lot of misunderstandings about how the Spirit of God works. This has nothing to do with popularity or titles. Why? because the actual church cannot be seen with the naked eye. Remember I said that the wheat and the tare look exactly alike but the Lord knows those that are his.

Let's talk about the operation of the Holy Ghost when someone receives the Holy Ghost.

One of the reason's that Jesus was crucified is because he was breaking some the Mosaic Laws. In one of the scripture Jesus enters the synagogue and heals a man on the Sabbath. But the Pharisees was watching to see if he was going to break the law on the Sabbath, because they wanted to accuse him. This man had a withered hand, but healing was not supposed to be done on the Sabbath day.

And he saith unto to them, is it lawful to do good or evil on the Sabbath days, or to do evil? to save life, or to kill? But they held their peace. (**Mark 3:4**) **KJV**

Under the Mosaic Law you couldn't do meager things as well.

As you can see these people were self-righteous but thy could not see themselves. They were concerned more about the keeping the law but had no concern love nor concern for their fellow man.

The prophet Isaiah had a vision concerning Judah and Jerusalem. God had nourished them, but that they had rebelled against him.

*Hear, O heavens, and give ear. O earth: for the Lord hath spoken, I have nourished and brought up children, and they have rebelled against me. **(Isaiah 1:2)KJV***

*To what purpose is the multitude of your sacrifices unto me? saith the Lord: I am full of the burnt offerings of rams, and the fat of fed beasts; and I delight not in the blood of bullocks, or of lambs, or of he goats. **(Isaiah 1:11-20) KJV***

Therefore, this is one of the reasons that God wrapped himself in a body and came down in the likeliness of sinful flesh.

And without controversy great is the mystery of godliness: God was manifest in the flesh, justified in the Spirit, seen of angels, preached unto the Gentiles, believed on in the world, received up into glory **(1st Timothy 3:16) KJV**

If you notice this scripture lets you know who Jesus was. Because it says Godliness is a mystery and that God was manifested in the flesh.

Who was manifested in the flesh? God in other words, this is supernatural and must be revealed to by the Spirit of God.

In John the 13th chapter Jesus is getting closer to his crucifixion and is preparing his disciples for what is about to take place, but they were not aware of what was about to happen. However, Jesus knew who would betray him in the beginning. Therefore, the devil had put it into the heart of Judas Iscariot to betray our Lord and Savior Jesus Christ. Moreover, Peter wanted to know would he be the one that would betray him.

The one that he would give the sop to, would be the one that would betray him. After he had dipped the sop, he then gave it unto Judas Iscariot, knowing what he was about to do.

The Lord knew in the beginning that Judas was a thief. This is the reason he allowed him to be in charge of the money bag. Why? I believe that he allowed him to take charge of the money, because if he was in charge of it then he could not steal it. However, the bible does not say why Jesus allowed him take on this particular assignment. But I'm sure there had to be a reason for this.

Also, at the last supper they washed each other's feet. This symbolizes how we should love one another, and also humble ourselves before the Lord.

Nevertheless, Simon Peter was the outspoken one out of all of the disciples. After Jesus had washed all of the disciple's feet, he preceded to wash Peter's feet as well. But when he attempted to wash them Peter responded by saying that he didn't want his feet washed.

Peter saith unto him, Thou shalt never wash my feet. Jesus answered him, if I wash thee not, thou hast no part with me. Simon Peter saith unto him, Lord, not my feet only, but also my hands and my head.

Jesus was also letting the disciples know that where he was going, that they could not come at that particular time. Peter did not understand why these statements were being made. He, therefore, wanted to know where was Jesus going, and why he could not follow him? Jesus was letting his disciples know that they would be with him eventually. He was also letting them know that if he didn't go away, the comforter would not come which is the Holy Ghost.

Thomas saith unto him, Lord, we know not whither thou goest; and how can we know the way? Jesus saith unto him, I am the way, the truth, and the life: no man cometh unto the Father but by me. **(John 14:5-6) KJV**

This particular scripture verifies what I had stated in the past. It lets us know that we cannot go directly to God, because we are not holy enough, Therefore, Jesus is our mediator between God and man. In the Old Testament the animal paid for the sins of the person, but in the New Testament Jesus became our mediator and is at the right hand of the Father praying for us.

And whatsoever ye do in word or deed, do all in the name of the Lord Jesus, giving thanks to God and the Father by him **(Colossians 3:16)KJV**

There is power in the name of the Lord Jesus, and the devil knows this, because he was in heaven and knows more than we do about how the supernatural world works. His job is to deceive you into believing a lie because he is the father of it.

Another thing that I want to discuss in this chapter will be the different operations of the Spirit of God.

There are certain things that are hidden from the natural man because they are spiritual discerned.

But the natural man receiveth not the things of the Spirit of God: for they are foolish unto him: neither can he know them, because they are spiritual discerned. **(1st Corinthians 2:14)KJV**

What is the meaning of the word discern? The meaning of the word in this particular scripture would be a person that is not ableto recognize, understand, or detect what is right or wrong in the spiritual realm

Another thing that we have to remember is that we are not just natural beings, because when God breathed into Adam became a living soul, therefore, our bodies will die but we will live forever. Therefore, when someone dies, they transition from one realm to another.

This is one reason why satin temps people to focus more on the earthily realm, because he knows that this is just a temporally place where we dwell.

First let's talk about the Corinthian Church. The city of Corinth was a Greek city state, but mostly Romans lived in the vicinity. Corinth was also a very prosperous place, because they had great seaports and lots of tourists and travelers came to the area.

The city of Corinth was a very wicked place. They, therefore, became uplifted because of their prosperity. In addition, they also participated in pagan worship, and would also sacrifice meat offerings to their false gods. In addition, they created temples for them all so. Furthermore, some of the people would participate in orgies and offer sacrifices to them as well.

If you notice you can see how satin attempts to duplicate everything that God does.

Paul traveled many places so that he could evangelize for the Lord. He sometimes would travel to some of these places on a ship, because they were so far away. In addition, he stayed with the Corinthian church, so that he could teach them the ways of the Lord. He also gave them instruction on how to live holy in this present world. But after his departure some of them would return back into sin and participating in their pagan worship.

(1st Corinthians 10:20) KJV

Can you imagine living in such a wicked environment, but you desired to live for the Lord as well? You have to remember that these people were babes in Christ, and they had been raised to serve idol gods almost all of their lives. They were also living amongst evil spirits. Therefore, this wicked environment probably caused their flesh to become very weak. It can sometimes be very challenging to walk with the Lord when you are around so many demonic spirits. Consequently, the flesh is very weak, and it is sometimes very challenging for a saint that is rooted and grounded in the Lord to endure such an evil environment. On the other hand this may not be true for everyone because we all are made different.

I can recall when I first started seeking the Lord, I had to live in an environment that consisted of a lot of temptations, not including dealing with my own unclean spirits.

It was very tempting for me to not pick up that liquor bottle after coming from a fiery service. However, a sister that witnessed to me suggested that I could come and live with her. This was one of the greatest blessing that had ever taken place in my life. What she knew about the Lord was poured into me because of this. But this didn't mean that I didn't make mistakes along the way, because I had to grow in Christ. I thank God for his grace and mercy.

Paul would receive letters pertaining to how the Corinthian church were not walking up rightly before God.

He received a letter stating that one man was sleeping with his father's wife, and that some of them that were married were not coming together with their wives.

Paul urged them not to have fellowship with saints that were fornicators, dunkers, and certain other sins. Furthermore, they were not to even eat with them. However, these instructions were for saints but not for the world. Moreover, the Corinthian church was very carnal and they also had divisions amongst themselves (**1ˢᵗ Corinthians 5) KJV**

What is the meaning of the word carnal? The meaning of the word carnal is worldly, fleshly, lustful and etc.

And I, brethren, could not speak unto you as unto spiritual, but as unto carnal, even as unto babes in Christ. I have fed you with milk, and not with meat: for hitherto ye were not able to bear it, neither yet now are ye able. For ye are yet carnal: for whereas there is among you envying, and strife, and divisions, are ye not carnal, and walk as men? For while one saith, I am of Paul; and another, I am of A-pol-los; are ye not carnal? Who then is Paul, and who is A-pol- los, but ministers by whom ye believed, even as the Lord gave to every man? I have planted, A-pol-los watered; but God gave the increase. So then neither is he that planteth any thing, neither he that watereth; but God that giveth the increase.

In this last verse you notice that Paul is using something in the natural to explain the spiritual. He is letting the Corinthian Church know that no matter how well they preach or teach if God don't give the increase it will not prosper. Paul was aware that God must set his approval on whatever they attempted to do. For without him they could do nothing.

Execpt the Lord build the house, they labour in vain that build it. **(Psalms 127) KJV**

This particular church could not take in the deep things of God as of yet, nor had they grown in the simple things. (**1ˢᵗ Corinthians 3:1-7) KJV**

During their coming together to worship, there was a lot of confusion that had taken place, and God was not pleased in the way that they were conducting themselves in his presence.

If someone that was unlearned came into the church and heard them speaking in an unknown tongue, they would believe that they were mad.

And without controversy great is the mystery godliness: God was manifest in the flesh, justified in the Spirit, seen of angels, preached unto the Gentiles, believed on in the world, received up into glory. **1Timothy3:16**

Consequently, the meaning of the word edify means to build, instruct and or to teach.

What does 1st corinthians 14 chapter means when it says that the saints should desire spiritual gifts? Well in this chapter Paul is speaking about the gifts of the Spirit, and that he that prophesy is greater that he that speaks in an unknown tongue. In other words, he is saying that there is no harm done if someone speaks in an unknown tongue, as long as there was an interpreter. **(1stCorinthians 14) KJV**

Paul was letting them know that when they did speak in tongues that they should do it as unto the Lord, unless there was an interpreter to interpret what they were saying. The reason for this is because the person is speaking mysteries. In addition, true salvation is a mystery, and this is why most people will not understand it. When you speak in an unknown tongue you edify yourself as well. But he that prophesy edifies the church. For if I speak in an unknown tongue my spirit prays all so.

I would that ye all spake with tongues, but rather that ye prophesied: for greater is he that prophesieth than he that speaketh with tongues, except he interpret, that the church may receive edifying. **("Corinthians 14:5)KJV**

Let the prophets speak two or three, and let the other judge. If any thing be revealed to another that sitteth by, let the first hold his peace. For ye may all prophesy one by one, that all may learn, and all may be comforted. And the spirits of the prophets are subject to the prophets. For God is not the author of confusion, but of peace, as in all churches of the saints. **(1st Corinthians 14:29-33) KJV**

How is it then, brethren? When ye come together, every one of you hath a psalm, hath a doctrine, hath a tongue, hath a revelation, hath and interpretation. Let all things be done unto edifying. If any man speak in unknown unknown tongue, let it be by two, or at the most by three, and that by course; and let one interpret. But if there be no interpreter, let him keep silence in the church; and let him speak to himself, and to God.

For ye may all prophesy one by one, that all may learn, and all may be comforted. And the spirits of the prophets are subject to the prophets. For God is not the author of contusion, but peace, as in all churches of the saints.

As you can see, that the scripture was talking about people that had already been born again or had received the Holy Ghost.

Did you notice that the word judge was used? That is because like I once stated that there are various types of judging.

*Wherefore, brethren, covet prophesy, and forbid not to speak with tongues. Let all things be done decently and in order. (**1ˢᵗ Corinthians 14:39-40) KJV***

*Wherefore I give you to understand, that no man speaking by the Spirit of God calleth Jesus accursed: and that no man can say that Jesus is the Lord, but by the Holy Ghost. Now there are diversities of gifts, but the same Spirit. And there are differences of administrations, but the same Lord. And there are diversities of operations, but it is the same God which worketh all in all. (**1ˢᵗ Corinthians 12) KJV***

For one is given by the Spirit the word of wisdom; to another the word of knowledge by the same Spirit; To another faith by the same Spirit; To another gifts of healing by the same Spirit; to another the working of miracles; to another prophesy; to another discerning of Spirits; to another divers kinds of tongues; to another the interpretation of tongues.

For as the body is one, and hath many members, and all the members of that one body, being many, are one body: so also is Christ.

Notice that Paul states that there is one body that has many members, and how the saints at Corinth were Gentiles carried away with dumb idols

First, I need to explain what this all means. If you notice in 1ˢᵗ Corinthians chapter 12 Paul talked about spiritual gifts. Then he goes on to say that no man can say Jesus is Lord but by the Holy Ghost.

The second thing that that he says, is that God is not the author of confusion, but of peace. This lets you know that there was a lot of confusion that this particular church had going on during their services.

The third thing that he said, is that speaking in an unknown tongue is unto the Lord. Why? Because speaking in tongues is a heavenly language that the natural mind cannot comprehend.

But if there was an interpreter that knew that particular language, they would be able to interpret the wonderful works of God, and what he is saying in the spiritual realm.

This is what took place in the Upper Room on the day of Pentecost. There were devout men from every nationality that heard what had taken place in the Upper Room. This is why they were amazed, because they heard them speaking in the language that they were born. Furthermore, the Corinthian church were gentles and not Jews. Therefore, this lets you know that Paul was talking to believers or people that had been filled with the Spirit of God. If you notice, he uses the words church when speaking as well. Then he goes to say that if any unlearned person were to come unto them and see them all speaking in tongues at the same time than they would say they were mad.

These were new saints and thy needed a lot of attention. Paul knew that he needed to be patient with them, because they were babes in Christs.

Paul was trying to be patient with them, and he desired to see them grow In Christ.

How is it then, brethren? When ye come together, ever one of you hath a psalm, hath a doctrine, hath a tongue, hath a revelation, hath an interpretation. Let all things be done unto edifying

On the other hand, you cannot receive these particular gifts unless you have been filled with the Spirit of God.

The only person that was born with the Holy Ghost was John the Baptize because he had to baptize Jesus. Paul also stated that tongues were to edify the inner man.

Now there are diversities of gifts but the same Spirit.

This means that these gifts are given after you receive the Holy Ghost and not before. Then he begins to name some of these gifts in the bible.

Furthermore, there are gifts that are without repentance. **(Romans 11:29) KJV**

Some of these gifts would singing, dancing, acting, artistic abilities, cooking, acting, sports, and various other things as well.

However, these are a few gifts that may come with the Holy Spirit just to name a few.

For to one is given by the Spirit the word of wisdom; to another the word of knowledge by the same Spirit; to another faith by the same Spirit; to another the gifts of healing by the same Spirit; To another the working of miracles; to another prophecy; to another discerning of spirits; to another divers kinds of tongues; to another interpretation of tongues: But all these worketh that one and the selfsame Spirit, dividing to every man severally as he will. (1ˢᵗ Corinthians 12) KJV

However, these gifts can only be given after you've been filled with the Spirit.

Moreover, all the body is one and hath many members. Just like your natural body has many members such as your eyes, hands, feet, head, legs, nose, mouth and etc. All the members being one body by the same Spirit.

This is why I need every part of my body, because each part is important no matter how insignificant it may seem.

I beseech you therefore, brethren, by the mercies of God, that ye present your bodies a living sacrifice, holy, acceptable unto God, which is your reasonable service. (Romans 12) KJV

For as the body is one, and hath many members, and all the members of that one body, being many, are one body: so also is Christ. For by one Spirit are we all baptized into one body, whether we be Jews or Gentles, whether we be bond or free; and have been all made to drink into one Spirit.

But now hath God set the members every one of them in the body, as it hath placed him.

Now ye are the body of Christ, and members in particular. (1ˢᵗ Corinthians 12:27) KJV

If you notice this is symbolic to how our bodies are made.

One of my sons called me the other day and stated that he had cut two of his fingers very badly, while he was attempting to cut some corn. These were very deep cuts. He preceded to say that you don't value your limbs until you don't have them anymore.

This is the same way that we take for granted our families, friends, food, and our bodies in this life.

Chapter 8

The Importance of Being Filled with The Holy Ghost

If ye shall ask any thing in my name, I will do it. If ye love me, keep my commandments. **(John 14:14)KJV**

Therefore, the building is not the actual church, but your body is where God wants to make his abode.

Remember in the old Testament God would dwell with them in the temple that was made with hands, but when Jesus died on the cross that all changed.

This does not mean that you should not fellowship. In Addition, we must feed our spirits just like you feed your natural man. We all need to be encouraged at times, because we are in an continues warfare whether you believe it or not.

Nor forsaking the assembling of ourselves together, as the manner of some is; but exhorting one another: and so much the more, as ye see the day approaching. **(Hebrews 10:25) KJV**

An example would be if you have a car you have to keep up the maintenance on it. But on the other hand, you wouldn't take your car to just any place. You may seek advice from a friend or investigate the dealer before taking your car there. Therefore, you should have more concern when it comes to dealing with your soul. Because your soul is more precious than silver and gold.

Keep mind the I said that you can use natural things in the world to compare with the spiritual.

But the comforter, which is the Holy Ghost,
whom the Father will send in my name, he shall teach you all things, and bring all things to your remembrance, whatsoever I have said unto you. Peace I leave with you, my peace I give unto you: not as the world giveth, give I unto you. Let not your heart be troubled, neither let it be afraid. **(John 14:26) KJV**

Consequently, what he really was saying is that even though I'm not going to be here with you physically, but I will be with you spiritually.

Another reason that we need the Spirit of God is so that we can bear fruit. The fruit of the Spirit would be love, joy, peace, long-suffering, temperance, and meekness.

The fruit of the Spirit operates during trials and tribulations, and not just when things are going well.

These particular fruits can be seen more by someone that God has made a drastic change in their lives. On the other hand, they will become an entirely different person. This is called is called being transformed.

This may not happen overnight, but God may have to put them in the fire to purify them, which is not a good feeling because of the pain.

The closer you get to God and learn his ways the more that you will love him, because we don't always know him the way that we should. However, we should not just pick up our bibles on Sundays, but we should study it on a constant basis. On the other hand, you have some people that desire to have more of God in their lives, but thy may not be in the right church. They may not be aware that this can have an effect on their spiritual growth, especially if they don't know that much about him.

There are some people that stay at a church because they were raised there, but they are not growing. This is not a good thing no matter how prosperous that you may become.

In fact, instead of bringing the church into our reality we leave the Lord at the local assembly.

We need to sanctify ourselves and our homes as well. In addition, God desires to be in our everyday lives. He wants you to allow him to be, your doctor, your lawyer, your way maker, your friend, and even your healer.

However, you can't bear these fruits unless you abide in him. Just like the natural fruit cannot bear fruit unless the fruit abides in the vine.

In other words, God is saying that you can't live right without him. Because without him you can do nothing. However, you should desire that the inner man be stronger than the natural man. Because, if you are not abiding in him, you are like a ship without a sail.

Some people are naturally nice and kind, but this will not get you into heaven alone. I'm are not saying that these things are not important because they are. But you can't work your way into heaven by just doing good deeds. In addition, faith without works is dead. You must have both faith and works but works alone will not cut it.

For by grace are ye saved through faith; and that not of yourselves: it is the gift of God: Not of works, lest any man should boast. **(Ephesians 2:8-9) KJV**

You see the word boast in the scripture above. Why is it there? Because It means just what it says. I In other words, when you get to heaven you won't be able to brag about how good of a person you her on earth were, nor will you be able to boast about all of the good deeds that you've done. Therefore, it will be by both faith and good works that you may enter into heaven. Besides, if that was the way that God allowed us to enter heaven then he would not get the glory out of our lives. How many times do you see the word I in this sentence?

Another reason that God does not allow us to work our way to heaven, is because flesh loves to boast, and it is not our friend.

It doesn't matter how good looking that you may think that you are, nor how intelligent that you may *be*, your flesh is still your enemy.

Paul said, yea doubtless, and I count all things but loss for the excellency of the knowledge of Christ Jesus my Lord: for whom I have suffered the loss of all things, and do count them but dung, that I may win Christ. And be found in him, not having mine own righteousness, which is of the law, but that which is through the faith of Christ, the righteousness which is of God by faith: that I may know him, and the power of his resurrection, and the fellowship of his sufferings, being made conformable unto his death; If by any means I might attain unto the resurrection of the dead. Not as though I had already attained, either were already perfect: but I follow after, if that I may apprehend that for which also I am apprehended of Christ Jesus. Brethren, I count not myself to have apprehended: but this one thing I do, forgetting those things which are behind, and reaching forth unto those things which are before, I press toward the mark for the prize of the high calling of God in Christ Jesus. **(Philippians 3:8-14)KJV**

Paul stated that he counted all things as dung. In fact, Paul was very educated, but when he found Christ, but this was not as much of importance to him, because God had called him to another that was mission more important.

This is why he stated that he counted all things as dung. Another word for dung would be crap, fertilizer, poop, manure, and feces as well.

Paul cared nothing about this world and the things in it, because he was on another mission.

Some people don't realize that there are two types of wisdoms. The wisdom of the world and the wisdom from. However, both of them are total opposites.

But the wisdom that from above is first pure, then peaceable, gentle, and easy to be entreated, full of mercy and good fruits, without partiality, and without hypocrisy. **(James 3:16-17) KJV**

For where envying and strife is, there is confusion and every evil work.

Moreover, this kind of wisdom is earthly and is devilish also.

There is another reason that we need the Holy Ghost in our lives and that is to bridle the tongue. Why? Because if you can bridle your tongue you can bridle the entire body, and it is the hardest part of the body to tame.

The natural world is the opposite of how the spiritual world is ran.

For in many things we offend all. If any man offend not in word, the same is a perfect man, and able to bridle the whole body. **(James 3) KJV**

Behold, we put bits in the horses' mouths, that they may obey us; and we turn about their whole body.

The bit is placed in the horse's mouth so that the rider can communicate the horse which way that he wants the animal to go.

This is how we should allow the Spirit of God to led us when to speak and when not to speak. But this may be hard task for most people especially if you are outspoken and love to speak your mind.

Even so the tongue is a little member, and boasteth great things. Behold, how great a matter a little fire kindleth! And the tongue is a fire, a world of iniquity: so is the tongue among our members, that it defileth the whole body, and setteth on fire the course of nature; and it is set on fire of hell. For every kind of beast, and of birds, and of serpents, and things in the sea, is tamed, and hath been tamed of mankind: But the tongue can no man tame; it is an unruly evil, full of deadly poison. Therewith bless we God, even the Father; and therewith curse we men, which are made after the similitude of God.

There are times that we're saying negative things out of our mouths. But your words are more powerful than you think, because we are also spiritual beings. In other words, the words that you speak can come into existence into the natural realm because we are not just natural beings.

Death and life are in the power of the tongue: and they that love it shall eat the fruit thereof. **(Proverbs 18:21)**

and we will have to give an account for every idle word that proceeds out of our mouths on judgment day. (Matthew 12:32-37) KJV

Do you believe that a person that is intoxicated, or on substances abuse will sometimes speak a sober mind?

I can relate to this, because before I knew the Lord when I was intoxicated, I felt as if I was a different person. This would cause be to say and do things that I would not ordinally. Consequently, this can take place because when you are intoxicated or high on some other substance, it can open your spirit up to other spirits. Moreover, I would sometimes say things, because the alcohol gave me boldness to say what was in my heart in the first place. Why? Because out of the heart the mouth speaketh.

We also need the Holy Ghost to help us love our enemies. Anyone can love their friends, but it takes power to love someone that you know that hate your guts. Furthermore, the Holy Ghost will give you power to do what you can't do on your own.

On the other hand, even after receiving the Holy Ghost you will have to yield to the Spirit, because the war does not stop.

Some people may ask the question why didn't the thief on the cross that was crucified with our Lord and Savior, need to be filled with the Holy Ghost?

You have to remember that the thief on the cross was born under the Mosaic Law, and so was our Lord and Savior Jesus Christ. Therefore, he could repent and believe in his heart.

However, the criminal that was on the cross knew that he deserved to be punished because of his sins, but he didn't believe that Jesus deserved to be crucified.

And we indeed justly; for we receive the due reward of our deeds: but this his man hath done nothing amiss. **(LUKE 23:40KJV)**

Then Jesus spoke and said that he would be with him in paradise on the same day.

Moreover, would you believe that even Jesus broke some of the Mosaic Laws? The reason that he broke them was because God was tired of the bulls and rams and the other rituals that they were doing at that time.

Jesus was also tired of the Pharisees and the teachers of the Law of Moses. These people were experts in the Law of Moses, but they could not live what they were teaching. They believe that they were better than other people and loved to be seen of men. In addition, some of the Jews didn't believe in him as well. In fact, these people had the Law of Moses, but they were self-righteous.

The Romans and some of the Jews wanted to kill Jesus as well.

Another reason that you need the Holy Spirit is because it is a comforter.

What is the meaning of the word comforter in the natural? It would be a person or thing that provides consolation. Also, the comforter in the spiritual realm strengthen the mind, strengthen the spirit, releases stress, is an encourager, a mind regulator, gives support, gives hope, relief from distress, is a healer, is a keeper, is joy unspeakable, and is quickening Spirit.

What's the meaning of the word quicken? The meaning of the word quicken means to make alive, or to revive something or someone.

But if the Spirit of him that raised up Jesus from the dead dwell in you, he that raised up Christ from the dead shall also quicken your mortal bodies by his Spirit that dwelleth in you. (**Romans 8:11) KJV**

What this is saying is that you must have the same spirit in you that quickened Jesus Christ. In order to be identified with him we must follow the example that he left for us to do.

We all know that life is sometimes hard and for some people they never get a brake because of it.

When I was in the world, I would find my escape in heavy drinking and trying to find love in the wrong places. Furthermore, we were made to serve God but if you don't serve him then you will turn to other sources.

Even after finding him you must still be careful that the cares of this world will not take your mind off of the Lord. Some of these things could be drinking, drugs, alcohol, sports, technology, money, materialistic things, people, or love of self. The reason that this happens is because we were created to serve the Lord. Consequently, whatever you are obsessed with is where your heart is.

The heart is deceitful above all things, and desperately wicked: and who can know it. (***Jeremiah 17:9)***

Keep thou heart with all diligence; for out of it are the issues of life. (**Proverbs 4:23) KJV**

What this is saying is that you must have his Spirit in you, in order to be quickened by the same Spirit that quickened Jesus after his crucifixion.

It is the Spirit that quickeneth; the flesh profiteth nothing: the words that I speak unto you, they are Spirit, and they are life. (***John 6:63) KJV***

Chapter 9

The Upper Room Experience in the Book Acts

The first chapter of Acts, takes place after the resurrection of our Lord and Savior Jesus Christ. In this chapter Jesus had been seen by the Apostles for forty days. But while in their presence he was speaking to them about things pertaining to the kingdom of God. In addition, he commanded them not to depart from Jerusalem but wait for the promise of the Father.

Until the day in which he was taken up, after that he through the Holy Ghost had given commandments unto the apostles whom he had chosen: To whom also he shewed himself alive after his passion by many infallible proofs, being seen of them forty days, and speaking of the things pertaining to the kingdom of God: And, being assembled together with them, commanded them that they should not depart from Jerusalem, but wait for the promise of the Father, which, saith he, ye have heard of me. For John truly baptized with water; but ye shall be baptized with the Holy Ghost not many days hence. **(Acts :1-9) KJV**

If you notice in this particular chapter, the comforter that Jesus had mentioned to the disciples in John the 14th chapter, is now being fulfilled.

And when he had spoken these things, while they beheld, he was taken up; and a cloud received him out of their sight. And while they looked steadfastly toward heaven as he went up, behold, two men stood by them in white apparel; Which also said, ye men of Galilee, why stand ye gazing up into heaven? this same Jesus, which is taken up from you into heaven, shall so come in like manner as ye have seen him go into heaven. **(Acts 1:9) KJV**

The disciples where at a Mount called Olivet when this took place, but afterward they returned to Jerusalem to wait for the promise of the Father, as the Lord had commanded them to do.

Who else was in the upper room with the disciples? Most people may not realize that Mary, which was the mother of Jesus and his brothers were assembled with the disciples in the Upper Room as well. (**Acts 1:13-14**)

There are two baptisms that's mentioned in the scriptures. One would be the baptism of the water and the other is the baptism of the Holy Ghost. In fact, you have a natural birth and likewise, there is a spiritual one also.

John answered, saying unto them all, I indeed baptize you with water; but one mightier than I cometh, the latchet of whose shoes I am not worthy to unloose: he shall baptize you with the Holy Ghost and fire. **(Luke 3:16) KJV**

John the Baptize was talking to the people and some of the scribes and Pharisees that were coming to be baptized by him in the Jordon river.

Of course, the people had never experienced what John was conveying to them about the baptism of the Holy Ghost. Why? Because Jesus had to be crucified and had to as-send back to the throne in order for this to take place.

After Jesus had mentioned to the disciples about them going to Jerusalem, to be empowered with the Holy Ghost, the disciples asked him was he going restore the kingdom of Israel.

Why did they ask this question? The reason that they asked this was, because after the death of Solomon his son Rehoboam succeeded and became king of Israel. But there was conflict that took place between him and the twelve tribes. Therefore, ten of the tribes decided to separate themselves and start their own kingdom. However, the tribe of Judah and Benjamin stayed under the leadership of Rehoboam, which was the southern kingdom. But the northern kingdom was the tribe of Israel. Whereby, Jesus came from the tribe of Judah, and this had to take place, because it was in the plain of God. Without this happening Jesus would not had been born, nor would we have had a savior to redeem us from our sins.

Notice in this scripture it's talking about someone that is baptized with the Holy Ghost and fire like they did in the Upper Room on the day of Pentecost, and not the gifts that come in the package with it.

Jesus also uses words such as power and fire when speaking about the Holy Ghost. What do you think about when you hear the word power?

This word means force, authority, strength, and might. An example would be like your cell phone. you can use your cell phone if Its charged, but when it's not you're no longer able to use it. What this is conveying to us is that you need the word with power, and not just the letter.

You need the of power of God to walk right and to talk right. In addition, it is the resurrected power that will quicken our mortal bodies when Jesus shall appear for his church.

Then returned they unto Jerusalem from the mount called Ol-l-vet, which is from Jerusalem a sabbath day's journey.

And when they were come in, they went up into an upper room, where abode both Peter, and James, and John, and Andrew, Philip, and Thomas, Bartholomew, and Matthew, James the son of Al-phae-us, and Simon Ze-lo-tes, and Judas the brother of James.

These all continued with one accord in prayer and supplication, with the women and Mary the mother of Jesus, and with his brethren. **(Acts 1:12-14)**

Mary the mother of Jesus was born under the Mosaic Law and a new covenant had taken place after Jesus was crucified. Therefore, Jesus family had to be born again just like you and I.

On the other hand, while they were in the Upper room they were not just there gossiping and being idol. but they were all on one accord continuously in prayer and making supplications unto the Lord. As you can see some powerful things can take place when we are all on one accord and have one mind. Therefore, this lets us know that even the ones that were In the upper room had to fight for the blessing as well. Moreover, there were about a hundred and twenty people that were the Upper Room. As a matter of fact, the Lord could've allowed them to be filled with the Holy Ghost immediately, but for some reason he didn't allow it to take place this way. **(Acts 1:15) KJV**

Whereby, where there is unity there is strength. This is one of the reasons that satin likes to bring division, among people. Likewise, division sometimes takes place in churches.

There was a group of people that attempted to build a tower up into the heavens. The name of the towel was called the Tower of Babel. However, during those times everyone spoke the same language and had all things in common. Nevertheless, God had to come down and confuse their language which made it impossible for them to accomplish their plain. In other words, when someone needed the material for building the towel, they could not understand what was being said. Therefore, this is showing the power of unity. **(Genesis 11:1-9) KJV**

Also, while Peter was in the Upper Room, he mentions to the people about how David prophesied about Judas betraying the Lord Jesus. Besides, every word of God is true. How do we know? Because whatever the prophets in the Old Testament spoke of came to pass in the New Testament.

An example of this this would be found in the *Isaiah 9:6 For unto us a child is born, unto us a son is given: and the government shall be upon his shoulder: and his name shall be called Wonderful, Counsellor, the mighty God, The everlasting Father, The Prince of Peace.* **(Isaiah 9:6) KJV**

Isaiah was a prophet that was born in the Old Testament, and he prophesied about the birth of Jesus Christ. Not to mention, that he talks about Jesus being God in the flesh. First, he states in the scripture a son would be born. Second thing that he says is that the government would be upon his shoulders. This mint that he would be hated by the system that he was born under. Therefore, this is one of the reasons that they crucified him. The third thing that Isaiah talks about in the scripture is that he called Jesus the mighty God, the everlasting Father, and the Prince of Peace. Consequently, Isaiah is letting us know that Jesus was God in the flesh.

While the apostles were in the upper room, they decided that they would seek the Lord on whom they should choose to replace Judas, because he had committed suicide after betraying the Lord Jesus. Therefore, the lot fell on a disciple by the name of Matthias.

I can't say how many days that it took for the promise of the Father to come to pass. But they were commanded by the Lord not to leave the Upper Room but wait for the promise of the Father.

It is a possibility that some of the disciples may have left the room, because it was approximately one hundred and twenty people that were in the room. Besides, some of the disciples may have gotten tired of waiting on the Lord, just like most of us do at times, especially when things don't happen as quickly as we may want them to. **(Act1:15) KJV**

The Lord didn't give them the exact timing that this miracle was going to take place, even though he could have, been testing their faith. It could've been that they might had to fight principalities to receive their blessing. Moreover, everyone may have stayed in the Upper Room and waited for the promise of the Father.

And when the day of Pentecost was fully come, they were all with one accord in one place. And suddenly there came a sound from heaven as of a rushing mighty wind, and it filled all the house where they were sitting. And there appeared unto them cloven tongues like as of fire, and it sat upon each of them. And they were all filled with the Holy Ghost, and began to speak with other tongues, as the Spirit gave them utterance. **(Acts 2)**

What does it mean when it states that the Holy Ghost came suddenly as of a rushing mighty wind? This means that they received the Holy Ghost full force just like a very heavy wind. In fact, you can feel Gods presence just like you can the wind but there are different degrees of it. Likewise, you can get a taste of heaven right here on earth.

But if you are so attached to this world, it could make it very difficult for you to experience what I'm trying to convey to you in this book. In addition, you don't have to be in a church building to experience what God has for you, because he can come where every you are. But you still need someone to show you the way, if you don't know the right direction to go.

So then faith cometh by hearing, and hearing by the word of God. **(Romans 10:17) KJV**

Therefore, you must seek the Lord not just while you are in a local assembly, but also invite him to dwell in your homes. Moreover, this is one the ways how you can keep your peace of mind.

Thou wilt keep him in perfect peace, whose mind is stayed on thee: because he trusteth in thee. **(Isaiah 26:3) KJV**

Sometimes we are perplexed in this life, because we fed our spirits too much negativity. We do this in various ways, without realizing what we are doing. Remember whatever you feed your spirit the most is what you will sometimes become. For example, if you feed your spirit negativity on a constant basis then you could become a negative person. However, if you listen to negative or satanic music you can draw negativity into your life also. Therefore, these spirits can cause you to become depressed, suicidal, bitter, negative, and have anger issues. This can take place because you have drawn negative spirits into your spirit. This can easily take place without you realizing what is going on, because you are not feeding your spirit with proper nutrition, which is the word of God and seeking his face.

The next thing that took place in the Upper Room is that they began to speak in cloven tongues as of fire, and it sat upon each of them. **(Acts 2: 3) KJV**

With the gift of tongues, you can somewhat control when to cut if off if you choose to, but when you are filled with the Spirit of God, he will totally take over completely. God will give you a sign to let you know that he is dwelling in your temple as well.

One example of speaking in tongues would be like when you purchased your shoes. You will notice that the tongues came with the shoes also. Likewise, when you purchased them, most people don't focus on the tongues inside the shoes. However, you assumed that the tongues are automatically inside of the them. Consequently, when you receive the Holy Ghost you should not focus on the tongues, but only on getting into Gods presence.

The next example of this would be like when you turn your faucet on in your home to get water. However, you have full control over the amount of water that you want to use. But when you are filled with the Holy Ghost it is the opposite of you being in control.

Have you ever opened up or shaken a soda that over flowed? Furthermore, it seemed as if it was coming out so fast that you couldn't control it. As a result, the soda may have spilled out all over the place. Likewise, this is similar to what it is like to receive the Holy Ghost. Its joy unspeakable and full of Glory.

Therefore with joy shall ye draw water out of the wells of salvation **(Isaiah 12:3) KJV**

I should let you also know that receiving the Holy Ghost is also a gift, but a different operation of the Spirit of God.

Acts 2: 4 says that they spoke in what they called clover tongues and they were all filled with the Holy Ghost and began to speak in other tongues as the Spirit gave them utterance.

What is the meaning of the word utterance? It means a spoken word, remark, or a statement. In addition, no one taught them how to speak in another language, because they were not doing this on their own. When God comes in the temple, he will speak out the it. If you notice the word Holy Ghost and fire are used interchangeable.

What does fire in the natural do? Fire purifies, gives heat, and spread. What does it mean when I say fire can spread?

This is saying in the spiritual realm that the Holy Ghost can fall from one person to another, if they desire it to.

I can recall, when one of my sons was approximately ten years old and we both were attending a powerful church service. All of a sudden, the presence of God fell on me. As a result, of him observing me the power of God fell upon him. Actually, this had never happened to him before.

However, there were devout men that could hear what was happening in the Upper Room and they begin to become confused.

There were Jews from Jerusalem and devout men, or religious men out of every nation that could hear what had taken place in the Upper Room.

These men were from different parts of the world, and most of them spoke different languages as well. But they knew that the people that were in the Upper Room were Galileans and didn't know their language.

Now when the message was noised abroad, about what had taken place in the Upper Room, it caused the people to become confused.

These devout men heard Jesus mother and brothers speaking in the languages that they were born.

And how hear we every man our own tongue, wherein we were born? Par-thi-ans, and Medes, and Elamites, and dwellers

In Mes-o-po-ta-mi-a, and in Judaea, and

Cap-pa-do-cia, in Pontus, and Asia, Phryg, and Pam-phyl-ia, in Egypt, and in parts of Libya about Cy-re-ne, and strangers of Rome, Jews and Proselytes, Creates and Arabians, we do hear them speak in our tongues the wonderful works of God.

It would be similar to a person that didn't know anything about another language, but someone from another country would be able to translate what they were saying.

And they were all amazed, and were in doubt, saying one to another, what meaneth this? Others mocking said, these men are full of new wine. but Peter, standing up with the eleven, lifted up his voice, and said unto them, Ye men of Judaea, and all ye that dwell at Jerusalem, be this known unto you, and hearken to my words:

For these are not drunken, as ye suppose, seeing it is but the third hour of the day.

But this is that which was spoken by the prophet Joel; And it shall come to pass in the last days, saith God, I will pour out of my Spirit upon all flesh: and your sons and your daughters shall prophesy, and your young men shall see visions, and your old men shall dream dreams:

And on my servants and on my handmaidens I will pour out in those days of my Spirit; and they shall prophesy:

And I will shew wonders in heaven above, and signs in the earth beneath; blood, and fire, and vapour of smoke: The sun shall be turned into darkness, and the moon into blood, before the great and notable day of the Lord come: And it shall come to pass, that whosoever shall call on the name of the Lord shall be saved.(Acts 2:12)KJ

Some of the people mocked them and stated that they must have been drunk or had been drinking new wine.

If you notice peter used the word drunken. Why do you think that he used the word drunken? He used the word drunken because they actually were drunk in the Spirit. However, when you get high or drunk in the world you open up the doors to satanic spirits. In addition, this particular high was created by satin, and he tries to duplicate everything that God has created, but it only leads to destruction. But this particular high comes from above and is joy unspeakable and full of glory. There's no high on this earth that can be compared to it.

When someone gets high in the world there's sometimes death in the cup. There are some people that cannot control themselves. They may conduct themselves in ways that they would not have ordinally.

Consequently, they may have damaged some valuable relationships that were important to them. They also, may have offended or even hurt someone physically, while under the influence of alcohol or drugs. However, the type of joy that comes from above is joy unspeakable and full of glory. Likewise, it also brings peace, and it is a comforter.

But Peter stood up and explained to the people and the devout men what had taken place inside of the Upper Room.

For these are not drunken, as you suppose, seeing it is but the third hour of the day. **Acts 2:15) KJV**

A lot of church goers never have experienced this wonderful experience, even though there are some people that don't really want to know about it at all.

One reason Jesus died on the cross is so that we can experience some of heaven right here on earth. He sometimes will even allow you to feel his presence, even if you are not living the way that you should. Why? It's because he loves us, and this is one way that he begins to deal with us.

Death could not hold Jesus body down in the grave. In contrast, he rose from the dead and is now at the right hand of the Father, making intercessions for us.

Because thou wilt not leave my soul in hell, neither wilt thou suffer thine Holy one to see corruption. (Acts 2: 27) KJV

Therefore let all the house of Israel know assuredly, that God has made that same Jesus, whom ye have crucified, both Lord and Christ. (Acts 2:36

Now when the devout men heard what Peter had said they were pricked in their hearts. This means that they had regret or became sorrowful for their sins. Then they asked Peter what shall we do?

Then Peter said unto them, Repent, and be baptized every one of you in the name of Jesus Christ for the remission of sins, and ye shall receive the gift of the Holy Ghost. (Acts 2:1-38) KJV

Repentance is a very important step in receiving the gift of the Holy Ghost.

What is the meaning of the word repent? It means to change one's mind. Also, to feel or express sincere regret or remorse about one's wrongdoing, or sin. In addition to turn away from it and surrender yourself to God.

This does not mean that it will be an easy task. One reason that it may not be easy is, because most people are programed as soon as they are born. In addition, the times that we are living in are worst, then it has been in the past and becoming more satanic as well. Likewise, now I understand how satin operates and can control people through this worldly system.

But the heavens and the earth, which are now, by the same word are kept in store, reserved unto fire against the day of judgment and perdition of ungodly men. **(2nd peter 3:7) KJV**

But the day of the Lord will come as a thief in the night; in the which the heavens shall pass away with a great noise, and the elements shall melt with fervent heat, the earth also and the works that are therein shall be burned up. (2nd Peter 3:10) KJV

God desires for us to prosper, while we are here on earth. But what he is saying is don't set your affections on things of the earth. Why? because we don't know what the next day will bring, and there is nothing in this life that is for certain. In addition, all things in this life are vanity. In other words, everything here on this earth is temporal or only for a season. But only what you do for Christ will last.

For what shall it profit a man, if he shall gain the whole world, and lose his own soul? (**Mark 8:36**) **KJV**

You may also encounter people that may not understand spiritual things therefore, they will not understand the journey that you are attempting to travel. Moreover, they will attempt or try to persuade you that you are going the wrong direction. Likewise, the Lord may not be dealing with them the way that he is with you. In fact, he may not have revealed certain things to them as well. As a result, they will not understand where you are coming from. On the other hand, this does not mean that you are any better than anyone else, because we are all in a warfare and no one has it made. However, it's by God's grace and mercy that we are not consumed. Another thing that I would like to mention, is that some people may not feel comfortable around you when you are attempting to please God. Why? Because the way that you are living shines on their darkness, and light and darkness will not mix. In addition, when you are living a sanctified life you can sometimes cause them to feel condemned about themselves. In fact, they may feel more comfortable around people that have the same spirit as they do. However, what does this mean? We are living in a time whereby you are persecuted for having your own identity. Why? It's because we are in the end time. This is called group think as well. I read on a website that this is a part of the satanic world as well. As a result, almost everyone, dresses alike, think alike, and eat the same kinds of foods and ect. Again, this is a part of how people are being programed, and there is a plain behind this.

One of the hardest things for us to do is to surrender ourselves completely to the will of God. I guess you say why?

For my thoughts are not your thoughts, neither are your ways my ways, saith the Lord. For as the heavens are higher than the earth, so are my ways higher than your ways, and my thoughts than your thoughts. (**Isaiah 55:8-11**)

What is the meaning of the word remission? Remission in the natural is something that is lessening, reduction, or decreases in something. However, in the spiritual it means to remove.

Therefore, we know that when someone Is buried in the natural that their entire body goes into the ground. However, in the spiritual realm the same should occur, because we are buried with him by baptism. Furthermore, this is one of the ways that we must be identified with him. In fact, there is no need of being baptized if you have not repented of your sins because it will be a waste of your time.

The bible also speaks about people having a form of Godliness but denying the power. Therefore, this is saying that a person can have the word of God but just the letter but no power. To sum it up, it may consist of formality, custom, rules and regulation, In other words you're just going through the motions but denying the power.

When you're walking with God it does not mean that you will not make mistakes, but it does mean that you will feel more of a conviction when you make them. Therefore, you can go to your heavenly Father, and ask him for forgiveness and more grace.

For the promise is unto you, and to your children, and to all that are afar off, even as many as the Lord our God shall call. And with many other words did he testify and exhort, saying, save yourselves from this untoward generation. **(Acts 2:38-47) KJV**

No matter what you may see other Christians do this will have nothing to do with your relationship with God.

I stated in the beginning of the chapter that the wheat and the tares look exactly alike, but when God comes, he will do the separating.

You should not just look at a person's title nor popularity and believe that they are of God.

Though I speak with the tongues of men and of angels, and have not charity, I am become as sounding brass, or a tinkling cymbal.

*And though I have the gift of prophecy, and understand all mysteries, and all knowledge; and though I have all faith, so that I could remove mountains, and have not charity, I am nothing. And though I bestow all my goods to feed the poor, and though I give my body to be burned, and have not charity, it profiteth me nothing. (1ˢᵗ **Corinthians 13) KJV***

*And they, continuing daily with one accord in the temple, and breaking bread from house to house, did eat their meat with gladness and singleness of heart, praising God, and having favor with all the people. And the Lord added to the church daily such as should be saved. (**Acts 2:46) KJV***

The meaning of the word doctrine would be their teachings, knowledge, Principles, and instructions.

The word church is used in this scripture, because the actual church is not the building, but our natural bodies, are the temple that God wants to dwell in for his glory. Also, God wants to use your hands, feet, your mind, and all of your member. Actually, we should not what to do our will. But we should desire to be in our Father's will which is in heaven.

Chapter 10

My personal Testimonies and Supernatural Experiences

I would dare not end this book without my giving personal testimony. Why? Because I've encountered so many supernatural experiences that I haven't shared with many people. Therefore, I must be a witness to some of the things that I've shared with you in this book. In addition, I would like to give God all of the glory. Why? Because It's not about us but It's about Jesus.

When you've had an encounter with God for yourself, no one can take that away from you. This is why positions has nothing to do with what I'm sharing with you. Some people may have good intentions and may also have been enlightened in certain areas when it comes to spiritual things. But there are different levels of what I'm trying to convey to you.

An example of this would be found in Matthew the 13th chapter, that pertains to the seeds that had been sewn by the sower. We have to remember that the word of God is like a seed that is planted. Therefore, one-person plants, another person may water, but God gives the increase.

This chapter will explain more indebt about what kind of heart or ground the word falls on. Therefore, some seeds fell by the wayside, some fell on stony ground, some fell among thrones, and others feel on good ground.

Jesus would sometimes use parables, to explain something that he was trying to convey to the disciples.

And when he sowed, some seeds fell by the way- side, and the fowls came and devoured them up. **(Matthew13:18:23)kjV**

An example, of this would be someone that hears the word of God but does not fully have an understanding about it.

Hear ye therefore the parable of the sower. When any one heareth the word of the kingdom, and understandeth it not, then cometh the wicked one, and catcheth away that which was sown in his heart. This is he who received seed by the way side.

I can somewhat relate to this scripture, because I had a similar experience before receiving the Holy Ghost. Furthermore, I didn't know that much about the word of God, nor did I understand spiritual things.

I would sometimes spend the night over my neighbor's house. This particular day there was a person that was there. She was there witnessing to my neighbor. However I don't want to mention what religion this was.

Therefore, the lady attempted to talk to me about her believes, and I in return mentioned to her about the Holy Ghost. Consequently, she stated that the Holy Ghost was not for the times that we were living in, but it was for Paul and some of the other patriarchs.

After speaking with this particular lady, there seemed to be a battle going on inside of me, and I became very confused and troubled in my mind as well. However, the Lord delivered me from this false spirit, that was trying to deceive me. I can't explain how it happened, but it did.

I could've been one of those that received the word by the wayside. But by God's grace and mercy it didn't take place what satin had planned.

The Lord was drawing me by his Spirit, even if I didn't know him, he knew me. He allowed various situations to arise in my life, but these were not ordinary situations.

The Lord knew that I needed someone in the flesh to guide me, and he allowed me to meet the right person at the right time. However, I could've rejected what I was being taught, but his sheep knows his voice, and a stranger they will not follow.

God allowed the heat to turn up in my life, so that he could use it to draw me. Therefore, this caused me to seek him not just at church but also at home. On the other hand, I practically lived in church. However, the times that we are living in now I can see everything that we were taught coming to pass.

In addition, he knows what each and every one of us will need to make this journey.

There were many days that I had to fight for the spiritual blessings that God had for me. In other words, I would call on his name for long periods of time until I reached his throne or got into his presence. This helped me to strengthen my inner man. Because I needed all the ammunition that I could get to make this journey. Besides, I'm not going to tell you that it was an easy journey because it wasn't. But God gave me a hunger and thirst for more of him.

Consequently, you must have a hunger and thirst sometimes before he will fill you with his Spirit. Because if you are hungry and thirsty it will motivate you to seek him more than ever. Furthermore, now I understand why the word says

*Blessed are they which hunger and thirst after righteousness: for they shall be filled. (Matthew **5:6**)**KJV***

Eventually, the Lord placed it on my heart to go on a three day and night fast. Why? Because, when you have strong holds in your life you can only be delivered by fasting and prayer. Moreover, there were many yokes in my life that needed to be broken. In addition, I also needed to be around people that allowed the Spirit of God to move freely.

I can remember the day that the Lord filled me with the Holy Ghost. Nevertheless, the church that God sent me to always conducted very powerful services. But this particular service was even more powerful. I therefore, believe that it was just my time to get my brake through. Especially after the long fast that I had gone on and my persistence. On the other hand, God is sovereign, and he still did not have to save me, but he did.

What does the word sovereign mean? It means that God does whatever he wants to when every he wants to. In addition, he is all knowing and all powerful and is in control.

In fact, during this particular service almost everyone was on one accord. In addition, no one simmered you down while the Spirit of God was moving upon you, nor did they rush the service.

I had felt God's presence many times before, but this time it was different. In other words, this was on another level.

All of a sudden, I saw a shadow coming toward me because I had reached another realm in the Spirit.

When I opened my eyes, I could hear myself speaking in another language that I had no control of. Besides, I wasn't trying to control it because it was such a wonderful experience. However, when I opened my eyes, I saw a light all around me. It was Gods shekinah glory. In addition, his glory filled the entire church. Even though people were in the mist the Spirit of the Lord was so powerful upon me, it was as if they were not there. In fact, it was as if my body was on earth physically, but my spirit had reached another realm.

After this wonderful experience had taken place, I noticed that I had moved from my seat, to the front of the church but I was not aware of ever walking across the flour. In addition, this showed me how powerful Gods presence is. However, our bodies could not take all of his power. Besides he only gives us a sample of what heaven will be like here on earth. As a result, of what had taken place when I went to go home, I noticed that everything that I saw when I went outdoors looked brighter than normal. I also noticed that the color of the trees and grass looked much brighter than before. I can't explain to you why. I'm only telling you what took place. "I looked at my hands and they looked new and I looked at my feet and they did too". Nevertheless. I didn't know that I had to be made and wasn't aware that this was just the beginning. Why? Because we were born In sin and shaped in iniquity, and we have to work out our salvation. We are the clay and he is the potter. In addition, I had to go through the fire to be purified, by test and trials.

I'm not going to tell you that you won't have to fight to stay with the Lord. Besides, anything worthwhile will not be easy of course, but it will be worth it.

I've received an infilling of the Holy Ghost as well. I believe the Lord had mercy on me and gave me the second filling, so that I would have enough power to go through the extreme tests that was to come. Furthermore, I was also in the fire at that particular time as well. However, the second filling was not on the same level as it was the first time. Why? I don't know. Consequently, I don't believe that I would have made it without the refreshing that God had given me, because I was going through so much in life.

I guess you can say everybody goes through something. This is true, but there are different levels of going through in this life. And there are people that hardly ever get a break, nor do they have a support system. This can make or break you. I guess I'll just say like the song says I Never Would Have Made It.

I dare not forget about another supernatural experience that I once had, while I was driving on the highway.

It was a normal day and I was at home when the phone rang. A family member called me stating that a young lady that once lived with me and my family over thirty years ago was in the hospital. She was a little older than I. She appeared to have had a difficult life and I as well.

I was anxious to go to the hospital to see her and to pray with her. I didn't know if this would be my last opportunity to ever see her again. However, she didn't know that I was coming to see her. Therefore, she was very surprised when I entered the room at the hospital. Therefore, I prayed with her and attempted to comfort her as best as I could. In fact, I had just brought a new car and didn't have enough driving experience. However, since I didn't know that much about driving, I probably should have had someone in the car with me that was more experienced.

On my way back home from the hospital I preceded to go on the highway. But then I noticed that I was lost. I believe that I was going approximately sixty-five miles per hour.

This made it even more freighting, because I was driving at a high speed, and it caused me to panic even more.

I therefore, began to close my eyes because of fear of not knowing where I was going. Likewise, when you panic you cannot think very clearly. Therefore, I proceeded to say out loud "oh God I'm lost"!

I don't know if my hands were on the steering wheel or not, because I had panicked and was not aware of my surroundings. In other words, fear had taken me over and had me under its control. I don't recall, if there were cars in front of me or behind me, because of the state of mind that I was in.

All of a sudden, a supernatural force that I could not see turned the steering wheel to the right side of the highway, and I could hear a screeching sound. In addition, I could see the steering wheel being turned on its own. However, as the steering wheel was turning, I quickly came back to my snice's and noticed a familiar exit sign. Thereby, I proceeded to go in that direction.

It was as if God had predestined for me to be at that exit that I was familiar with. In fact, he knows everything before it is going to happen.

On the other hand, God is soverent and does whatever he chooses to and do whatever he pleases. This could have gone in many directions, I therefore, could had died, or killed someone else.

I love the Lord because he heard my cry, and it is not because we are worthy of his goodness and his mercy. For all have sinned and fallen short of the glory of God. Therefore, I will praise him no matter what other's may say or do, because he is worthy of my praise. I can't speak for no one else. I'm crying right now because I can feel his presence while writing this book. Moreover, other people may write about success and how great they are, but the greatest person that I have ever known is the Lord Jesus Christ. There's none like him. Because all flesh is as grass, but my God will never fail.

This book may not be for everyone, but there is someone out there that wants more of God and is tired of going through the motion.

We are in the last of the last days and time is running out for all of us. Life is much more than money, cars, and material things. The things that we see on earth are only for a season and they are only temporal.

For what will it profit a man to gain the whole world and lose his soul, or what will a man give in exchange for his soul.

God is giving us warnings after warnings. All you have to do is look at the weather and other signs that he is allowing. It is time to awake out of sleep for the day is at hand.

I know that people are saying it is global warming, but even if it is God is allowing it. Also, there are a lot of other supernatural things that are going on because most people are not aware of it.

The night is far spent, the day is at hand: let us therefore cast off the works of darkness, and let us put on the armor of light. **(Romans 13: 12) KJV**

Therefore, you can't believe God if you don't believe that he is a rewarder of them that seek him. Also, you can't go by what you may see, feel, hear, and what others may say and do.

In the book of Hebrews there are many examples of people that had to walk by faith and not by sight.

The book of Hebrews talks about how Abel offered unto God a more excellent sacrifice than Cain.

God told Noah to build an Ark because it was going to rain. It had never rained on the earth before, therefore the people that was around Noah thought that he was losing his mind.

Remember the bible says that there is nothing new under the sun and the same thing will happen again, but next time the world will not be destroyed by water but by fire. **(2nd Peter 3:7)KJV**

By faith Abraham, when he was called to go out into a place which he should after receive for an inheritance, obeyed; and he went out, not knowing whither he went. **(Hebrews 11: 8) KJV**

It was by faith when God told Abraham to offer up his only son and he obeyed him. In fact, Abraham had to be tested before he would be called the father of many nations. There are times in our lives when things will sometimes seem to get worst before the blessing.

By faith the harlot Rahab perished not with them that believed not, when she had received the spies with peace. **(Hebrews 11:31) KJV**

A lot of people do not know the nationality of Jesus. The word of God says that he was a Jew and the son of David.

In Matthew the first chapter it tells you some of the genealogy of Jesus. It mentions a harlot that was named Rahab, and Jesus was in her family tree.

In these modern days a harlot would be called a prostitute, but in biblical days they were called harlots.

Rahab's people were enemies of the Israelites and she lived in the land of the Canaanites. However, Rahab changed her life and the Lord blessed her mightily for it.

This lets you know that Jesus does not see as man see's, but he died for all sinners as well.

We were born in sin because Adam and Eve sinned in the Garden of Eden. They, therefore placed everyone that was born under condemnation. Therefore, God cursed Adam because he listened to his wife. He also cursed the ground and stated that in sorrow shell, he eat of it all the days of his life.

This is one of the reasons that God didn't except Cain's offering in the book of Genesis because he brought fruit of the ground and the Lord had cursed it.

This is why we must be born again because we were born into the state of sin.

The wicked are estranged from the womb: they go astray as soon as they are born, speaking lies. **(Palms 58:3-11) KJV**

Being a morally good person has nothing to do with what I'm talking about.

For all have sinned and come short of the glory of God.

This is why we must be born again from above and be transformed by the renewing of our minds.

We are more than just humans in a body, but we are also eternal beings with an inner man. Even if you don't believe it now you will soon find out. Because ever knee shall bow, and every tongue shall confess that Jesus Christ is Lord.

Are you wondering why you are not growing spirally?

Do you wonder why when you attempt to do what is right that you end up doing the opposite?

Do you desire to know more about Gods presence and his word as well?

Do you feel as if something in your life is missing even though you may be blessed materialistically?

Do you say I don't have time to read the bible because your too busy?

Do you read the bible but can't seem to get an understanding about what you've read?

Do you feel as if you want to learn about God's ways but have not one to teach you?

If you desire a deeper relationship with the Lord, then this book is for you. On the other hand, reading this book will reveal some things about God that you may have never known. Furthermore, it will reveal to you things that came from the Spirit of God as well. And if you have never read the bible, this book is for you as well. In fact, this book will open up your understanding about spiritual things in the unseen world. You also need to know who your real enemy is, and this book will teach you that. Moreover, this book will also enlighten you on why you need to fight the flesh, the world, and the devil. In addition, it will teach you how you can get to know God instead of knowing about him as well. You're also learn how God operates in the spiritual realm.

This is what you will learn after reading this book.

- The Different Operations of the Holy Spirit
- The Importance of Being Filled With the Spirit of God
- The Upper Room Experience

Biography

Her name is Francine Harris. The meaning of the name Francine is free one.

She was born in Richmond Virginia. Her father was in World War 11. Her mother's name was Irene Robinson, and her father's name was Troy Lee Robinson. Her mother's name was Irene Katy Jones. She was told that her father named her after a young lady that he knew in France. Francine lived part of her life in Philadelphia, and the other part of it in Richmond Virginia as well.

She loves to exercise at the gym and study on how to stay healthy as well. In addition, she spends a lot of her time studying the word of God and seeking him for more knowledge.

She didn't realize that she had a passion for writing until she attended college, she later found out that writing was something she loved to do in her spare time. In addition, after taking an entrance exam for a community college she remembers receiving a letter in the mail from them. The college suggested that she should take some classes in writing, because they were impressed with how well her writing skills were on the entrance exam. what she had written on the entrance exam.

She also made the dean's list several times while attending Sojourner Douglas College. Now at the age of 68 she still will not give up on improving her life. On the other hand, she has been saved for 45 years and have seen many miracles in her life as well. She dares not say that she has not made some mistakes along the way, because this would be a lie. But God has been very patient and is a merciful to all of us. For all have sin and fallen short of the glory of God. But because he is merciful does not give us a right to trample over his love.

She will be sharing many more books in the future as well.

Dedicated to

Elise Duncan is a poet. She has written a book and the name of it is called "Divine Destiny Making a Difference in Poetry". Thank you for your support.

My sons Warren, Benjamin, Cortez, Curtis, Ryan, Jeremy.
My daughter in laws and grandchildren.

Bishop Michael Fields (Refuge Temple Church)
Bishop Douglas Williams
Elder and Sister Plummer (True Apostolic Church)
Sister Bonita Hunter (My old Prayer Partner for many years)

The Substitute Teachers, and Ms. Hendricks, at Northwestern High School. MS Violaine, Dumorne, a school counselor.

My Son Dion Robinson and Shirley Robinson (Deceased)
My Husband Benjamin Harris (Deceased)
Sister Stella Robinson (The sister that brought me to the Lord) Deceased.

Substitute Teachers at Duval High School located in Maryland, Froilan Brwason, Xlibris and staff

Book Edited by Francine Harris

Email Frannymay5152@gmail.com

I dare not end this book without showing my appreciation to my sons Jeremy Jamin Harris, and Benjamin Harris because I had lost the motivation to finish this book.

But the Lord used them to encourage me to keep it moving.

Pictures Done by My Son Jeremy Jamin

I would suggest that you read the King James Bible when attempting to learn the word of God. I guess you say why? The reason that I'm saying this is because some of these new translations are changing the word, from its original state. An example would be in Matthew 8:23-27and Mark 4:35-41. This scripture talks about when Jesus calmed the sea while he and his disciples where on a boat, and the sea was boisterous as well. One of the new translations are now stating that he called the disciples cowards, because they were afraid of the boisterous storm. Jesus never called anyone a coward in the scriptures. Furthermore, it is human nature for humans to be afraid when things in this life catch you off guard. In addition, in biblical times they didn't use modern day terms. On the other hand, the way that it should be written would be

And he saith unto them, Why are ye fearful, O ye of little faith? Then he arose, and rebuked the winds and the sea; and there was a great calm.

It should not say why do you cowards have so little faith ? Would you believe that some of the latest versions now have the word police written in them? an example of this would be Acts 16: 32-35. This scripture is talking about Paul and Silis when they were in prison, because of their love for God. But an earthquake took place while they were there, but a supernatural thing took place. Their chains were also broken from off of their bodies.

There are many more strange changes in most of these particular bibles. Most people don't see any harm in what has taken place. Why? Because you must remember that the word of God is supernatural and must not be tampered with. Also, God told us not to take away from his word, and if anyone did that they would receive the plagues that are written in the book. In addition, their names would be taken out of the book of life.

If you don't own a bible you can go to site called Bible Hub or BibleGateway as well. There are approximately 50 or more bible's versions on their sites. If you want to verify what I have just written, you can use the site called BibleGateway. First, you may go on Bible Hub and pull down all of the versions at once and compare scriptures. Moreover, on this particular site you will see the words Parallel, Sermons, Topical, Strong, and Comment written next to one another. Next you should go to the word that says Parallel, and there you will find all of the new versions of different translations of various bibles. You may have to go through more than one version to verify the things that I'm saying to you, because I didn't want to name what bibles that I found this information from.

I also, didn't capitalize the word satin in none of my writings. Why? Because he gets no glory from me.

The KJV bible may not be popular in today's standards, but I must not change the word of God in any shape nor form.

This book is summarized by teaching you about the Tabernacle, which was under the Mosaic Law. It explains the meaning of some of objects that were there, but they had a symbolic meaning. Moreover, you will understand why God was not happy with the Mosaic Laws. It will also explain to you the meaning of sanctification, and why we must be sanctified as well. You will see why Abraham and the some of the other patriarchs were so important in the scriptures. In addition, this book will explain to you the proper way to be baptized, and prepare you for the indwelling of God's Spirit, and why you need it. You will also know what to expect when it takes place. Besides, this book will teach you the importance of repentance before you're baptized. In addition, you're understand how to be identified with Christ when he comes back. Likewise, you're understanding of what strongholds are in the spiritual realm and how to free yourself from them. In fact, you're learn about what kind of angel satin was before he fell. Another, thing that you will learn from reading this book is how fasting and prayer can give you power with God. In addition, you're learn the proper way to fast. You're also learn how to do warfare with the flesh and the devil. Moreover, this book will teach you more in dept what took place in the Upper Room. Also, it will explain to you who was there. Then it will explain to you why this particular book is so important. Consequently, I've written down scriptures so that you can verify what I have written. Equally important, you're learn the different operations of the Spirit of God and how he operates in the spiritual realm. You're learn about the different gifts that are in the body of Christ. This book will teach you about the Corinthian Church and why Paul wrote some of the things that he did about judging. It will teach you various kinds of judging that are biblical. I also wrote some of my own supernatural experiences in this book as well. May the peace of God be with you all.